JEWS AND AMERICAN COMICS

JEWS AND AMERICAN COMICS

An Illustrated History of an American Art Form

EDITED BY PAUL BUHLE

THE NEW PRESS

NEW YORK
LONDON

Requests for permission to reproduce selections from this book should be mailed to: Permissions Department, The New Press, 38 Greene Street, New York, NY 10013.

Published in the United States by The New Press, New York, 2008
Distributed by W. W. Norton & Company, Inc., New York

LIBRARY OF CONGRESS CATALOGING-IN-PUBLICATION DATA
Jews and American comics : an illustrated history of an American art form /
edited by Paul Buhle.
    p. cm.
Includes bibliographical references.
ISBN 978-1-59558-331-4 (hc)
1. Comic books, strips, etc.—United States—History and criticism. 2.
Comic books, strips, etc.—United States. 3. Jewish cartoonists—United
States--Biography. 4. Jews—United States--Intellectual life. 5. Jewish
wit and humor, Pictorial—History. 6. American wit and humor,
Pictorial--History. I. Buhle, Paul, 1944-
PN6725.J49 2008
741.5'973089924—dc22
          2008018479

The New Press was established in 1990 as a not-for-profit alternative to the large, commercial publishing houses currently dominating the book publishing industry. The New Press operates in the public interest rather than for private gain, and is committed to publishing, in innovative ways, works of educational, cultural, and community value that are often deemed insufficiently profitable.

www.thenewpress.com

Book design and composition by Lovedog Studio
This book was set in Fairfield Light

Printed in Canada

10 9 8 7 6 5 4 3 2 1

Contents

Acknowledgments

Foremost thanks go to the artists and scriptwriters who contributed their work to this volume. May the memory of those gone serve as inspiration and may the living prosper in their art.

Along my own path of fifty-some years, through childhood devotions, learning about comics, writing about them, and editing them, a handful of friends, not all of them artists or Jewish, have been hugely helpful with their insights and good spirit: Dave Wagner, Jay Kinney, Ben Katchor, Lewis Leavitt, Danny Czitrom, George Lipsitz, Robert Crumb, Harvey Pekar, Penelope and Franklin Rosemont, Leonard Rifas, and James Danky. Most especially I want to thank my active collaborators in creating comics, including Gilbert Shelton, Dave Wagner, Harvey Pekar, Gary Dumm, Nicole Schulman, Peter Kuper, Sabrina Jones, Nick Thorkelson, Spain Rodriguez, and Sharon Rudahl. Hats off to Thomas LeBien, at Hill and Wang, as well.

This volume could not have been completed without the Yiddish translations by Eddy Portnoy, the arrangements for reprinted material from a number of artists made by Denis Kitchen, the editorial guidance of Marc Favreau, the copyediting skills of Aja Pollock, the production oversight of Maury Botton, and the painstaking work of Jason Ng.

JEWS AND AMERICAN COMICS

Introduction

JEWISH COMIC STRIPS? JEWISH COMIC BOOKS? THESE IDENTIFI-
cations would have seemed forced only a decade or so ago, possibly anti-
Semitic a few generations earlier. Yet the personnel of the comic book trade
have been historically Jewish, and the lineage of the single most successful
print phenomenon arising out of that trade, *Mad* magazine, is no mystery to
anyone. But as in films and television, if along a somewhat different time-
line, Jewish artistic self-identification has been late in coming. Success,
through at least the 1960s and sometimes far beyond, lay in assimilation.

We have now entered different times, for which *Jews and American
Comics* can represent a sort of vernacular summing up, as well as an exploration of artistic richness underappreciated nearly up to the present. The
work of artists in the pages to follow offers no comprehensive collection.
Little-remembered artists and some famous ones, timid about their Jewishness, remain to be identified or rescued from obscurity and ethnic anonym-
ity. Published volumes by the most famous, from Al Capp to Ben Katchor,
are now readily available, not to mention the treasure trove of comic images on the Web. But here in this volume can be found, for the first time, a
wide-ranging selection that identifies continuing themes of Jewish-related
content and certain artistic approaches sharing more than the artists themselves often recognize.

Self-recognition and wider recognition did not exactly begin yesterday. The first comic strip artist to win a Pulitzer Prize *for his comics* is Art Spiegelman, whose *Maus*, in two volumes, has gained him lasting international fame.[1] The first comic artist to win the prestigious MacArthur ("Genius") Grant for a comic strip, Ben Katchor, has been described by Spiegelman as the "most Yiddish" of artists, although Katchor's work is in English or a semi-English of immigrants in vanished or imaginary neighborhoods. Among the most successful and most admired members of the younger generation, for his screenwriting as well as his comics, is Daniel Clowes, whose work is frequently on view in the pages of the *New York Times Magazine*. The underground hit of the 2003 film season—winner of awards from the Cannes Film Festival and the Los Angeles Film Critics Association, among others—was *American Splendor*, by no means the first film ever based on comic strips but the first to combine the originals (i.e., the people on whom the characters are based), the actors playing them, and animated characters based upon them all on the screen. *Splendor*'s creator, Harvey Pekar, might have disappeared from the earth thirty years ago and still been remembered in a footnote for his early role in the career of Robert Crumb, one of the totemic figures of comic art. Gentile-born, Crumb is Jewish by way of ambience, with Jews as not only his frequent subjects but his friends, wives, and children.[2] And this is only a small part of the large, often enigmatic story, including a footnote to history known only to specialists: the first paperback original *with original art* is 1959's *Jungle Book*, an artistic triumph and commercial failure by *Mad* founder Harvey Kurtzman, who is acknowledged as one of the greatest architects of modern comic art.

THE SYSTEMATIC STUDY OF COMIC ART IS RECENT.[3] Within the last decade, more published volumes about comic art, of both the scholarly and picture-book variety (the latter often boasting the superior research), have been produced than in all the previous history of the subject. The nineteenth-century roots of the comic strip, explored by very few scholars decades ago, have begun to emerge, shedding light on both precursors and the rich outpouring to follow. Very much like Yiddish literary culture, the story goes back to European origins, then develops new contours along with a large new readership in the "new country," the United States. As Yiddish began to fall away, American comics began to have a huge impact on European (and other) comics, a phenomenon renewed and reinforced by the wildness of the 1960s and 1970s undergrounds, whose spawn definitely include Spiegelman, Katchor, and, by extension, many a young Jewish comic artist today—even, one might add, those who claim to have broken the link between narrative and drawing decisively, creating, as Chris Ware has memorably proposed, a comic art for its own sake.[4]

No two scholars are likely to have the same precise definition of a comic strip, but the sequential narrative running across several or many panels ("boxes") remains the obvious beginning spot. Illuminated religious texts seven centuries ago already had such panels and even an inclination toward the humorous and grotesque. But the emergence of a mass (and predominantly lower-class) audience craving entertainment offered the possibility for the modern comic strip to take form and for a certain kind of artist to make a living. Technological advances naturally played a key role, with the first glimmer of the modern strip appearing during the early decades of the nineteenth century, when drawings could be transferred to lithographic stone and set in print.

The steady evolution of the comic strip would need to be explored, in a detailed way not yet attempted, through a larger history of visual storytelling. The artist or illustrator has almost always needed to self-train, certainly until recent generations. Much as the shift from silent to sound movies did for screenwriters, changing technology compelled successive reorientation for comic book creators, with much of the learning process taking place on the job. Prestige has been rare, rarer than material success. And curiously, hostility toward the comic strip ran parallel, during a crucial phase, to the contempt of Jewish elites for Yiddish: disdain for the comic strip as a "bastard form" merging picture and word was not so far from the charge of *jhargon*, a language neither Hebrew nor German nor Russian but something in between, leveled against Yiddish. Especially in an age of ascending romantic nationalism, such a description was certain to mean something unclean. That both comic strip and Yiddish literature were deeply vernacular, appearing (in Yiddish theater, books, and the daily or weekly press) around the same historical moment, is arguably no coincidence. A buyer had been created for the seller.

One might suggest a further similarity between the two, as some English-language Jewish comic strip artists themselves have done. The advance of photography, to quote a scholar of the comic strip, plunged "the viewer into hyper-vision, into an unknown world, the world of speed . . . concentrated energy into a flash of time," inspiring the vernacular artist to do likewise for his readers.[5] The early comic strip artist was in vital ways a cousin of the early filmmaker, and occasionally (through animation) a filmmaker himself. Comic strips *about* movies naturally sprang from artists' tools during the 1910s, as movies were to spring from comic strip characters not long after, and animated films emerged as a new art form.

The other decisive connection between Yiddish and the comic strip goes straight to humor, whether as social commentary or unadulterated "fun." The legendary qualities of Jewish humor cannot be well documented before the nineteenth century, and early popular Yiddish writers like Mendele Moykher Sforim and Sholem Aleichem seem to have stylized their folksiness to suit their potential readership.[6] But behind the poses, beneath the unresolved mystery of origins, there was always a sense that the punishment inflicted upon the Jews, threats to their livelihood or lives, and the simultaneous traditions of literacy and *pilpul*, the question-and-answer dialogue of Hebrew schooling, produced tragic comedians and also the lighter sort. Humor was a way of making life bearable and also understandable.

Jewish humor thus reflected something not so common to all cultures, the articulation of resentment by the dispossessed against the elite. The pressures for compulsory religious orthodoxy and acceptance of the predominating social influence of merchants and rabbis were not so terrifying as contemporary reality and the still more dire threats of Gentile persecution to come. But they may have been more irksome on a day-to-day basis, coming as they did from other Jews. Sholem Aleichem and Mendele Moykher Sforim actually built upon a history of shtetl jokesters when they deployed satire to score political points, above all the need for collective self-education and a better sense of the outside world. But they were imaginative writers as well. In the voice of their precursors, a sort of nontheological mysticism offered a counternarrative, closer perhaps than anything else in Jewish life to the carnivals held by the Gentiles (with furtive Jewish participation), turning all the social rules upside down for a short time. The raucous laughter of the vulgar crowd at the mockery of kings and religious leaders presages, at any rate, printed Jewish humor attacking politicians, the rich, and the get-along-go-along rabbinate. The *Purim Shpiel* or Purim Play, the source of all Jewish theater, was more reverent—but who knows if folksiness did not sometimes suggest more in the body language of actors and their sideways glances at the crowd.

Darker theories about the kinship of Jews and comedy or humor developed in the cerebral corners of anti-Semitism in the last third of the nineteenth century, i.e., shortly after Jews began leaving the pale in larger numbers and making their presence felt in European capitals. According to some scholars and much popular literature, the expulsion of humor, satire, and general merriment to the literary gutter was associated with the connection of Jews and sexuality—just as Jews would be associated in the popular anti-Semitic mind with the "jungle music" of jazz in the twentieth century. True humor, according to the guardians of genteel culture, was transcendent by nature. The Jew is thus confined to uncreative mockery.

Just as women were considered inveterate liars, using a secret language to disguise their disconnected (or irrationally connected) memory and mentality, as the theory went, so Jews had a *Mauscheln* ("Moishe Talk"), a unique but by no means admirable way of expressing their own disconnectedness and their sense of being lost within history. Otto Weininger, the most noted of the anti-Semitic Jewish intellectuals, granted that Jews had great talent for all manner of superficial arts, but reasoned that this merely compensated for their lack of depth—that is, their inability to create real art. Essentially nonbelievers (Judaism could not be granted status as a real religion), they were hypercritical of everything, mere cultural parasites upon civil society and the arts wherever they gathered and expressed themselves.[7]

Not only Gentiles believed such slander. A less malignant version of this bundle of ideas was common among assimilated middle-class Jews, most especially in Central Europe. Jewish intellectuals were probably happy about the natural increase of the European Jewish population from the eighteenth century onward but resentful of the fact that the vast majority, an increasing majority, was Yiddishist—i.e., vulgar—and perhaps hopelessly so. The very point of the Haskalah, a Jewish movement that was a late variant of the Enlightenment, was to strip off most of the baggage that poor Jews carried over from centuries in the shtetl. Freud himself, until the rise of Hitler, declined to attribute anything higher than "wit" to a Jewish writer.

Sander Gilman concludes that the Jewish desire for flight from one's body into the whiteness of the Gospels' soul prompted a wish for invisibility.[8]

Invisibility would, of course, be a natural desire for European Jews entering the age of the Holocaust. But within American mass culture, two generations of Jews had already made their splash as comedians of practically all kinds, especially the reputed lowest kinds, in movies, radio, and comics. The overwhelming majority were indeed, by their own choice, most often invisible—as Jews.

If Yiddish and heavily accented English might be taken as the real-life version of *Mauscheln*, then the "invisible" Jews of the 1930s and 1940s among the artist-writers of nonhumorous comic strips and comic books were still more perfect masters of self-disguise. Comic-page jokester characters who made fun of everything were more than likely to be dyed-in-the-wool Jewish "types," whether they used the word "Jewish" or not. The severest critics of both forms were by no accident often the respectable Jewish classes, who, like the owners of the *New York Times*, naturally felt that a serious and rational approach to the world had no place for such nonsense as the comic strip.[9]

There is no identifiably Jewish comic-page "look." Art varies with the artist, although it has been argued that many Jewish artists over several centuries have literally "seen" reality in special ways. We could add to this suggestion more definite but apparently unrelated symptoms of a distinctive Jewish folk art, such as the nonuse of bright yellows, reds, or greens in familiar peasant costumes, shtetl Jews employing in their place the darker hues, grays and blacks; or Jewish folk and modern artists' similarly persistent use of the word and the letter, whether Hebrew or Yiddish, as an art object *in itself*. According to other arguments, even the supposed Jewish perspective in a certain kind of modern photography may be part of the story, literally a way to see the picture. These matters pose near-imponderables that we may nevertheless take pleasure here in pondering. So infrequently has the vernacular been approached in Jewish terms, so shameful was the vernacular considered by Jewish elites and upwardly mobile intellectuals until recent decades, that there is more than ample room for useful speculation.[10]

At any rate, the revolutionary energy of modern art from the 1910s to the 1930s among Jewish easel artists, set and costume designers for the stage (not at all excluding the puppet stage), book illustrators, and others seemed to go in the same thematic direction. That surge of energy moved toward creation in the scattered but intense global world of *Yiddishkayt*, a common Jewish life and culture outside the familiar frameworks of religion or the state. This modernist shift constituted, all in all, a project with nearly everything going against it. What had seemingly been solid in Jewish life for centuries was melting away at a ferocious pace, and no one knew what would replace it.[11]

The pace of the industrialization, urbanization, secularization, and immigration that began during the last decades of the nineteenth century was being accelerated enormously. Radical and revolutionary doctrines, from Communism to Zionism and many in between, took hold because solutions were desperately needed, and not only because of the swift rise of anti-Semitism in Europe and elsewhere. *Something* was required to define the Jewish self while Jews entered modernity at every level, as overrepresented in the creative arts as they were underrepresented in country clubs and other preserves of the aristocracy, whether European or American.

For these purposes, the comic strip fit perfectly, and more than fit. In the comic *book*, it could be seen as ideal, not because comic books attracted any critical admiration—during the decades of newspaper superiority in the information marketplace of daily life, they attracted considerably less than the lowly "funny pages" comic strip, in fact—but because the Jewish role in the comic book was both extensive and intensive. Nowhere but Hollywood, and mainly behind-the-camera Hollywood, was the Jewish role so influential in a major form of popular art. But just as Los Angeles could never be as Jewish as New York, the movies could never be as Jewish as comic books, which, irrespective of actual images that were almost entirely Gentile, were produced *by* Jews for the masses. In the longer run, with the emergence first of film and then comics as accepted art forms, Jewish images would be "outed" by the intentions of the creators and with the assistance of critics and approval of the audience. Long before that, the conscious and unconscious identity of the artist had manifested itself, reached out to readers who saw in some version of comics the refracted representations of themselves.

It would be a mistake, of course, to isolate the Jewish-created comic from other expressions, low and high, of Jewish artists in the age of comic book glory. But it would be a far greater error not to identify the comic as *the* vernacular form in which Jewish genius (or, at least, the genius of some hundreds of Jewish artists) found its true mass audience. This art developed by phases, responding to readers (and markets) but also responding not infrequently to impulses within modern art and to the terrible dilemmas of the age. Hackwork and denigrating racial characterizations, hyper- (or pseudo-) patriotism—all can be found together in vast abundance, and they are noted here in passing. Real popular art and a sense of social conscience are more rare but far from absent, their presence associated most strongly with Jewish artists, Jewish scriptwriters, Jewish publishers, and, although we can't prove the case, probably an intense Jewish readership as well.

We know far more about one very particular but crucial case. Thanks to a proliferation of semischolarly volumes and fanzines and the availability of reprints, EC Comics, the innovative publisher of the early 1950s that must be considered the grandest aesthetic experiment in comic book history, has gained at least a significant fraction of its deserved status.[12] Nowhere else in the history of comics, or at least in the history of American comics until around 1970, did the form so evidently gain what has been called a "reflexive" character: self-conscious experimentation with the readers' perception of form as well as content. Nowhere was the commercialization of society so ferociously attacked, not even in Theodor Adorno's famed dialectical screeds. Nowhere, finally, did the tragic view of organized society—epitomized by warfare but also realized in nonutopian futures of alienation and post–atomic war efforts to survive and perhaps rebuild—attain such vivid expression. On that last point alone, in the world of the mostly Jewish, liberal-leaning science fiction writers, EC had not so much rivals as collaborators, including that famed Gentile Ray Bradbury, his writings a great favorite story source for EC's artists and scripters.

In this respect as well, it does no disservice to either side of the studio-art-versus-comic-art debate to compare, for instance, the finest comic artists to the sociopolitical and artistic efforts of the Soyer brothers, Ben Shahn (whose 1940s war posters fairly well epitomized the step forward in accessibility from 1930s lithography), and Jack Levine. To capture the Jewish world's passing but still on hand in older Jews and older neighborhoods was a task that now required a different vocabulary from the comics.

The search for spiritual roots, especially after the realization of the Holocaust, would grow more vital. Once the vernacular had been introduced (or reintroduced since the days of that Baltimore-born Jewish American Dadaist Emmanuel Radnitzky, who became a Parisian and called himself Man Ray), it was not going to vanish.[13]

In the process of finding and keeping an audience, generation after generation of Jewish comic artists helped define what each stage of Jewish life in the United States might be. They were and are Jewish Americans, not just "Americans," and their claims are not tied to religion or state (the United States or Israel). They are what they are—as seen, sometimes more keenly than elsewhere, in the eye of the comic artist who does not need to flatter elites or place himself upon the pedestals of the Louvre, or, for that matter, MoMA.

IN HIS FAMED BOOK OF ESSAYS *About Looking*, John Berger quotes popular philosopher Max Raphaelson as suggesting that art is a way out of the "world of things," through an aspiration to create a "world of values" in its place. Berger goes properly onward to discuss Herbert Marcuse, the great rebel Jewish mind of the 1950s and 1960s who likewise viewed art as a "Great Refusal" of existing society and its miseries. Then Berger adds his own pained reflections. Before World War II, great art was able to bridge a gap between "what was and what could be," or at least bridge it in anticipation. Since the horrors of the Holocaust and atomic warfare—twin signs of ultimate inhumanity and the threat of total destruction—"unity in a work of art [is] inconceivable," and "the moral concept of the Impossible" arises as it could not earlier.[14]

Inasmuch as Berger was writing specifically about René Magritte, and by extension the surrealists at large, his dating could be interrogated as somewhat inaccurate. The impossible arose in the world of rebellious art in response to the horrors of World War I, but also in response to the romantic impulses drawn from the theories of the distinctly unromantic Sigmund Freud. According to the surrealist rewriting of popular cultural history, the great comic strips always dealt with the world of the impossible, a Rube Goldberg world that satirized its real-world counterpart.[15]

The overarching argument of this book, demonstrated vastly better in pictures than in the editor's words, is at root that Jews have for a century been on an extended journey to find themselves. As artists or readers, they have very often found themselves in a seemingly unlikely spot: the comic strip. The search has, of course, only begun.[16] One might describe what you see here as a continuation of a project—largely if never entirely unconscious until recent times, when it gained severe consciousness—almost as daunting as the stabilization of *Yiddishkayt* before the end came. Look carefully, reader, Jewish or Gentile, and you may find yourself, too.

צווישען פרעה'ם

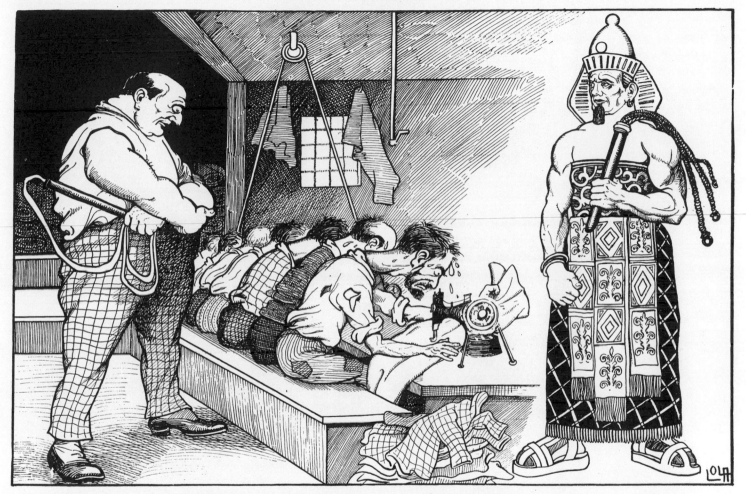

פּרעה מלך מצרים: ביי מיר האָבען דאָך עפּעס אויך אַמאָל אידען געאַרבייט אָבער אַט אַזוי אַ? — ניין!...

"Between Pharaohs," in the *Groyser Kundes*, 1911. The Pharaoh of old looks at the Jews of the twentieth century and says, "Jews once worked for me in Egypt, but never like that." The new taskmaster looks Jewish, mirroring a commonplace reality in the needles trades. The artist is Lola, aka Leon Israel.

"Pa-ayper-Reggs" by Pekar and Crumb, from *The New American Splendor Anthology* (New York: Thunders Mouth Press, 1993). A recuperation of a Jewish past fast slipping away, and the oral historians, interviewer/scriptwriter, and artist rush to capture the ambience. Reprinted with the permission of the writer and artist.

"The Jew" by Art Young, from *Good Morning* magazine, 1921. In the face of rising European anti-Semitism and the first American Red Scare, the leading socialist comic artist of the 1910s–20s Left hails the reality of Jewish accomplishment.

Chapter 1

YELLOW PRESS HEADLINERS: JEWISH COMICS IN THE DAILIES

A NATURAL SITE FOR THE TALENTS OF JEWISH IMMIGRANT YOUNG-sters in great American cities taking in the popular art around them, the daily newspaper was not, for generations, anything like an open road to Jewish American success. Unlike films, the tabloid world was already well established by the time most Jews arrived and learned the English language. On the other side of the ocean, Germans and Englishmen, among other Europeans, had forged ahead in comics, some of them bringing their talents with them to the new land. This chapter is the briefest in this book, and for good reason. But it explores what was an important start for the genre in several key respects, as well as the end of the short-lived Yiddish-language-comic-strip genre.

Between Jewish and Yiddish comic strips and their respective artists, we could perhaps make one primary distinction. For educated, assimilated Jewish Americans, the comic strip provided a guilty pleasure at best, an embarrassment at worst, offering further evidence (along with "Hollywood," meaning films) of cultural philistinism, vulgarity sans the dirty words. The Jewish but emphatically English-language comic strip artists, several of them beloved by the masses, could hardly be seen as avant-gardists, whatever their personal opinions of art and life. They were simply toilers in the field of popular culture.

Within the cultural ghetto of the Yiddish world, things looked very different. Some of the rebellious young literati known as *Di Yunge* actually wrote for the ghetto comic weekly the *Groyser Kundes*, and others wished that they could, in place of their own mostly blue-collar jobs. The same writers also took up with the Yiddish dailies, their prose and poetry appearing side by side with the most popular fare, a relation natural enough because they shared the limited audience of Yiddish readers. Yet the *Kundes* remained unequalled in its visual *Yiddishkayt* (that is to say, Yiddishness). It was also arguably the most unique American comic weekly in any language, as well as the precursor to *Mad*—but no one outside the Yiddish world would know. If the youngest readers of the *Kundes*, before it closed its doors in 1927, were perhaps the eldest readers of *Mad* when it opened its own doors in 1952, no one has recorded the evidence.

The Yiddish comic strip was as rare on the printed page as the Yiddish political cartoon was overrepresented in abundance and quality, a visual high point of any daily in the language. Rare, that is, but not insignificant. The first important Yiddish comic strip artist is doubtless Samuel Zagat. Creator of several strips over the course of the 1910s that were published in the *Varhayt*, the *Jewish Daily Forward*'s main competitor during these years, Zagat launched *Moving Pictures*, in effect a visual exercise like those in the English-language pages, including Winsor McCay's *Little Nemo* above all. Zagat continued to experiment, eventually formulating a favorite figure, Gimpl Benish the matchmaker, who was apparently an instant hit. Here every possible gender-relations gag could be exercised, and plenty of commentary could be made about the "characters" in the condensed world of New York immigrant Jewry.

Almost never is Gimpl successful in his strained efforts, perhaps because the pairs of souls he tries to unite evidently do not really want to be mated. Since the popular culture of "romance" sweeping across everyone in the city contrasted so heavily with the more fatalist (often more clearly patriarchal) matches set from time immemorial in the shtetl, confusion was inevitable and humor was a way to deal with the widespread sense of disorientation. Frequently, Zagat dispensed with the matchmaker formula entirely and Gimpl became an almost normal comic strip character, distinct as an urban ghetto type. The artist thereafter abandoned the comic strip form entirely, making his living mainly by drawing political cartoons and supervising the artwork in the *Daily Forward* until his death in 1964. For decades, possibly on the sly, he also drew illustrations for the *Forward*'s opponents on the Left, notably the communist-oriented *New Masses*, under a pseudonym.

The takeover of the *Varhayt* by the *Tog* in 1919 underlined the microcosmic quality of the literary ghetto and the constraints upon its professional cartoonists: now there were only two large, commercially viable Yiddish dailies in New York. In contrast to the *Forward* and the *Tog*, which themselves merged generations later, the *Tsayt*, a Labor Zionist daily, lasted a mere twenty months, from 1920 to 1922. Zuni Maud, the *Tsayt*'s house comic strip artist, was less a professional, more a bohemian destined for a life of poverty and radical attachments. Born in Poland in 1891, he came to New York in 1905 and, while working in a cigarette factory, began attending various art school classes, including those of the radical Ferrer School, at night. An intimate of *di yunge* litterateurs, he was likely the most junior staff member of the *Groyser Kibitzer*, which morphed into the *Groyser Kundes*. Maud was also surely the comic artist most influenced by the contemporary Ash Can School, not only because he actually studied with Robert Henri and George Bellows but because the crossover between cartoons and paintings had been clearest and most effectively realized in the *Masses* (1911–17) before its wartime suppression by the Wilson administration. The eldest of the *Masses* artists, beloved socialist cartoonist Art Young, had been the master of crosshatching in the 1890s style, and here, too, influences upon Maud can be found. These could also be found far outside the Left, as in Bud Fisher's famed *Mutt and Jeff* strip, which featured two racetrack touts who became emblematic of contemporary urban types in early animated film as well as comic strips.

Maud's *Tsayt* strip *Tsharli, Vas 'maskhste* (Charlie, What Are You Up To?), which dealt with the dilemmas of the new immigrant in particular, might have appeared in any of the Yiddish dailies. But his character Tsharli, like the paper itself, seemed to cling to the existence of an identity endangered by assimilation, the editors perhaps indulging their cartoonist's artistic freedom. At the end of this run, the *Tsayt* nearing collapse (and with it, the artist's salary), Maud invented the autobiographical character within the strip, a style that would remain practically unknown among cartoonists until the underground cartoonists of the 1960s and after made it almost standard.

The reason for this innovation, beyond sheer creative energy, was the intimacy of the audience, as in later underground newspapers—the comic catered to a counterculture so small that artist and reader shared a way of looking at the world, one utterly contrary to the dominant view. Tsharli (likely a reference to Charlie Chaplin, widely thought to be possibly Jewish, something the orphaned Londoner refused to deny) tells his *Tsayt* editor not to call him Tsharli anymore, because he does not want to be called an American, goyish name. With the end of the *Tsayt*, the Yiddish comic strip proper was finished. Tsharli was no more. Like so many Yiddish artists, Maud continued casting about for a form that suited him and allowed him to make a living. He found it in a uniquely Yiddish spot: the Modikot puppet theater, an international troupe with its own expressionist sets and costumes (Maud's work) and the jokes of his chief collaborator, fellow artist Yosl Kutler. Maud was still drawing cartoons (not comics) for the Yiddish left-wing daily *Morgn Frayhayt* into the 1950s, two decades after Kutler was killed in an auto accident, prompting a massive funeral turnout in New York. They had been real stars in their own small world.[1]

The Yiddish comic strip, as a form, was already outdated because of its near-total absence of dialogue bubbles.[2] Yet its lively characters and their actions were very American. It may be said to be the metaphorical *zeyda*, or grandfather, of the Jewish comic artist's emergence, as *Yiddishkayt* is for Jewish American popular culture. Jewish artists had more luck in the comic pages of the mainstream English-language press; they were never numerous, but several of the small handful revealed a certain genius.

Harry Hershfield was the first real star. A total celebrity in New York from the 1910s to the 1940s, he was a nightclub regular, he wrote a hilarious celebrities newspaper column, and out-of-towners could hear him on the radio as well as read his funnies and his joke books. Born in 1885 in Cedar Rapids, Iowa, to middle-class parents from Russia, he successfully placed his first strip, at age fourteen, in Chicago, where he moved; he then went off to San Francisco, came back to Chicago, and went on to his destiny at the *New York Journal* in 1910. *Desperate Desmond*, launched in 1910, satirized the entire genre of melodrama, from the nineteenth-century stage to dime novels and early silent cinema. The artist, finely talented at crosshatching and shading, was also inclined to experiment with collage, reflections on other comics of the day, and whatever came into his fertile mind (and pen). In 1912, he introduced a detective character suitable to the narrative framework: Dauntless Durham of the USA, an improved Sherlock Holmes, younger, more handsome, still pipe smoking. It was an extended riff on the silent-film melodrama but also on the further origins of the genre: the cheap theater and literature. Durham, the spotless hero, takes on Desmond ("You cur!") day after day, defending fair Katrina from marriage proposals and worse. Characters wear funny as well as fashionable clothes, make word and sight gags, and sometimes threaten to get involved in national and international politics. Foiled, Desmond somehow always gets away to return in the next strip. One might suggest that Hershfield was styling the satires of mass culture clichés that would appear in *Mad* two generations later. Naturally, everything would have to be reinvented.[3]

Hershfield hit his career stride in 1914 when a character out of *Dauntless Durham* acquired his own strip: Abie Kabibble, or Abie the Agent. A quarter-century later, Abie was still going. Hershfield meanwhile began a short-lived animation career in the late 1910s, did gag strips and half-page fillers for the press, spent time on his celebrity pursuits, and even, for a little while, worked as a story department head in Hollywood.

But Abie was his standby, and Abie was deeply, lovably immigrant Jewish as no comic character was before or has been since. A little guy with an oversized head, he craves success in American life but has no ill intentions, desiring not money so much as the symbols embodied in his successfully wooing "Reba, mine gold," the sophisticated flapper who was an ardent caricature of Hershfield's real wife (a sometime comic artist herself). Clumsy in social affairs, Abie is most in his element selling the "autermobile," notwithstanding a perfect absence of knowledge regarding a car's mechanical operation. He's Willy Loman as the American success story without the failure and accompanying pathos, adultery, and regrets.

Scholars of Hershfield's comic art over the years will quickly discover that the playful visual experimentation of Hershfield's early work disappeared within a decade, and that the artist settled down to what sitcom writers call "character maintenance." Within the saga of broken English and Jewish talking-with-the-hands gestures, a generation's tale was becoming old news. From at least 1930 onward, the drift toward assimilation completed itself, and even the signature accent disappeared. Early on, Hershfield seemed to have a premonition of this when, charged (by the precursor of the Anti-Defamation League) with encouraging popular anti-Semitism, he very correctly explained to a Chicago women's club in 1916 that Abie was the veritable refutation of the hook-nosed swindler or cheat stereotype. Like Abie, he wanted to be accepted and had the right to be accepted as a good American.

Rube Goldberg, born in 1883, grew up a middle-class San Franciscan. By contrast to Hershfield, he got a college education drawing for the *Pelican*, a then-new Berkeley campus humor magazine. Trained as an engineer, he acquired the fascination with machinery that became his comic livelihood (and led the *Oxford English Dictionary* to define a "Rube Goldberg" as a needlessly complicated, ultimately crazy device). Shortly after graduation, he joined the *San Francisco Chronicle*. By 1915, in New York, he earned almost two million dollars per year for syndication and books. It was a staggering accomplishment for the funny pages, where competition was fierce and editors heartless. Goldberg barely held himself back from a career in animation, where he doubtless would have played a central role as well. As it was, Hollywood's slapstick comedy reputedly borrowed much from Goldberg's strips. Dada's emerging avant-gardists, at the close of the 1910s and the other end of cultural creation, had already claimed him for themselves by exhibiting examples of his work. He does not seem to have coveted the honor.

By the mid-1930s, the drift of strips toward realism, or perhaps just his advancing age, evidently wore down the wild edges of this inveterate producer. He kept his Sunday work going, with an entire weekly newspaper page of gags and puzzles. He also played cameos of himself in films and turned himself finally to the editorial pages, drawing political cartoons against the fascist menace, and after the war won a Pulitzer. At eighty, he remade himself as a sculptor and became a towering figure within the National Cartoonists Society (they named their leading award after him). Beloved but never taken seriously as an artist except by his colleagues, he was just the great Rube.[4]

Only Milt Gross rivaled Hershfield and Goldberg, drawing more than a half-dozen syndicated strips simultaneously. More an author-artist, Gross made his literary splash with *Nize Baby*, a collection of his self-illustrated

New York *World* dialect pieces. A true and lifelong New Yorker of proletarian origins, born in 1895, he started out as an office boy at the *World*, soon became a protégé of then-famous artist T.A. Dorgan, and by twenty was working at the rival *New York Journal* with his own comic strip, about a loony sports fan. By the early 1920s he dipped his toes into animation with the same character, and he went on to do a dozen more animated cartoons in the same silly vein before shifting back into print (at the *World*) and offering his own spin on the Yiddish dialect, which had already proved so successful in Abie the Agent. Unlike the other Jewish comic giants, he became a prolific literary gagster, mostly but not entirely through reprints of his zany prose and doggerel poetry. "Hiawatta witt No Odder Poems" was doubtless his apex, and not so much poems as pictures and burlesque Longfellow dialogue; Indians and Jews had been linked comically in vaudeville for decades, and the link would last into television sitcoms, until it became an embarrassment.

The mediocre reception of Gross's graphic novel *He Done Her Wrong* (1930), arguably the first graphic novel ever (it was certainly the first in the United States), must have been a big disappointment. Thereafter, Gross devoted himself once again to the funnies, in Hearst's *World*. *Count Screwloose of Tooloose*, *Dave's Delicatessen*, and *That's My Pop* were worthy successors to his 1920s strip *Banana Oil*, which supplied the phrase that was the day's equivalent of "bullshit." *That's My Pop* was actually turned into a radio program (with Gross scripting) and his media career arguably extended itself to its limits with two animated adaptations in 1939. In 1945, he suffered a heart attack. Perhaps he had worn himself out. In semi-retirement, he managed to create a series called *Milt Gross Funnies* in 1946–47, certainly among the more bizarre comic books in an age when superheroes were growing stale and experiments were beginning to bring new life into the field. It is worth noting that the age of accents was over for him by that time, too.

The heavily assimilated Jewish comic artists of the next generation, few of them in the ranks of successful professionals, largely abandoned the affable craziness of the first generation. Ham Fisher was as assimilated as his name, with a backwoods WASP boxer, Joe Palooka, for his protagonist.[5] The Gentile model for the Jewish artist of the realist age, Milt Caniff arguably reinvented the continuity adventure strip. Ohio-born, he worked his way through college as an artist for the *Columbus Dispatch* and placed his first syndicated strip in 1932. He got his big break a couple of years later, coming up with an Orientalist-themed action strip that had added sex appeal: *Terry and the Pirates*. Roy Crane's *Captain Easy, Soldier of Fortune* had already set the motif in place, and Caniff contributed new skills, with the kinds of cinematic techniques that would soon serve Will Eisner well. The Dragon Lady, a slanty-eyed, sexy exotic who ran a mob but craved Terry, gave the strip its erotic angle. World War II, which found Terry in the air force, lifted the artist to previously unimaginable heights of popularity, and to a kind of antifascist idealism that meshed perfectly with the realism—at least for the comic pages—with which he presented the conflict.[6] To be generous, Caniff had created the war style of comic, full of generalized pathos and civilian suffering, that Harvey Kurtzman and others would adapt for still better purposes. Caniff was headed in another direction.

In 1947, as the Cold War heated up, Caniff left Terry and created a new strip, *Steve Canyon*, about an air force officer whose specialty would eventually become CIA-style operations in the Third World. This extension of the old imperial Great Game in pulp literature and in the life of real empires, with antifascism replaced by the steely determination of American operatives to rule the planet one way or another, lasted far longer than Caniff's stint on *Terry and the Pirates* but hit a bump by the late 1960s. The emergence of the civil rights and peace movements, not to mention generational rebellion and youth culture, posed problems with no solution for the talented artist. As disillusionment with the Vietnam War spread, the derring-do of Steve Canyon seemed to capture perfectly what was repellent about American arrogance, emphatically including the role of the secret government military operations once seen as romantic and dashing but now seen as global dirty tricks. As Martin Luther King Jr. led a generation of peaceniks, Caniff remained utterly baffled that Americans, young people especially, could be against the war for any reason—except when it wasn't successful. Conservative dailies along with liberal ones followed their readers' sentiment in dropping the strip, a remarkable development in a world where characters like Snuffy Smith drifted on decades after their creators had died and their social logic had disappeared. More to the point, the contrast with the glory days of Hershfield, Goldberg, and Gross could hardly have been greater.[7]

Ham Fisher's sometime assistant Al Capp, the creator of *L'il Abner*, was an assimilationist of a different type. In his imaginary town of Dogpatch, ethnicity disappeared only to make an occasional cameo appearance. By 1937, *L'il Abner* reached 15 million readers, and it would eventually reach 70 million. Capp had the will and the clout to win control of his strip from the syndicate, something unprecedented, and he thereby put himself in line to become the merchandiser of his own goods. Among the most popular were dolls and assorted objects bearing the Shmoo, a bloblike character who would supply humans with anything they requested—a super New Dealer or welfare-state socialist par excellence.

Here and there, into the lives and dialogue of the most unlikely Jewish space in the whole country, Capp introduced a handful of Yiddishisms and semi-Yiddishisms, and an occasional Brooklynesque character. Perhaps he was paying homage to his birthplace. Relishing his role as an outsider on the inside, Capp enjoyed tweaking leading personalities, especially conservative ones, well into the 1950s. His character General Bullmoose was a stand-in for a General Motors executive known to symbolize corporate heartlessness, and Capp made the most of it, thumping greed for money, power, and extended life (Bullmoose slept in a freezer). A decade later, stung by the counterculture and antiwar sentiment of the 1960s, Capp turned on his heel and became a crusading Goldwater conservative. It was an odd and, to be generous, a very late shift, though perhaps not so strange for a generation with swift upward mobility.[8] *Li'l Abner*, drawn by a variety of hands in later decades, was for many male readers probably most notable for exhibiting the mega-bosomy look of contemporary Hollywood productions. But in theme and style, it seemed more and more of an anomaly, a glimpse in the rearview mirror of comics at their last golden age, during the New Deal.[9]

Will Eisner, who invented a technical solution to this last problem, was yet another type, son of an apprentice muralist in Vienna who became a Yiddish set designer in New York en route to a mostly unsuccessful business career. Young Eisner aspired to be a painter, but also a successful businessman. He found his opportunity in commercial illustration and his calling in the new field of comic books. In the late 1930s, Eisner and his partner Sam Iger practically invented comic "packaging," a garment-district-style operation that created finished goods to be sold under the name of this or that pulp publisher. Always looking a step ahead and thinking about his own artistic talent, Eisner sold his comics interest and formed a company in order to distribute his own new strip, *The Spirit*, as a sixteen-page supplement to dailies.

The Spirit was an instant success in 1940, although a modest success: syndication Eisner-style never approached the success of Capp or Caniff. Eisner was, however, an overnight *makher* of the reinvented comics trade by virtue of his narrative and drawing style. Like Caniff's Terry but with less melodrama and ego, and vastly more humor and verve, Eisner's character easily survived the artist's induction into the army and brought forward new talent. Before his exit from the trade in 1952, Eisner employed, taught, or influenced a generation. Jules Feiffer, who apprenticed to Eisner in all but name in the years shortly after the war, has reminded comics fans that Eisner was best, finally, at the street-level view of New York lower-middle-class and working-class life.

One could not call that street-level view "Jewish," and yet, for the kind of comics reader who never failed to recognize contemporary film star John Garfield as Jewish, the ambience was evident and marked Eisner's work. Amazingly enough, even as *Mad* magazine, with its barely disguised Jewishness, advanced during the 1950s, the funny pages of American papers were still a *Judenrein*, or Jewless world, with the square-jawed Anglo-Saxon males and dainty females of Steve Canyon's domain arguably the most WASPish of all. Not until the 1970s did Jews begin to become more Jewish in the daily press, and for most of the time since, Jewishness has remained the same: the quirk of a particular quirky character. Unlike comic books, where the occasional Jewish superhero could be found, mostly during the 1980s and after, superheroes in the dailies remained, like Peter Parker (aka Spider-Man), identified by angst rather than ethnicity.[10]

Over the generations, Yiddish characters like Tsharli and broken-English Jewish immigrants like Abie the Agent had yielded to Americanization and their artists to the Americanizers. But never entirely. Soon, the Jewish face would be seen again.

THE BIG STICK

אַ זשורנאל פאר הומאָר, וויטץ אין סאַטירע

דריטער
יאהרגאַנג

פּרייז 3ס.
אוינסער נייאָרק
4 סענט

New York, April 7, 1911   VOL. III. NO. 14   נ‏‎יו יאָרק. דעם 7טען אַפריל, 1911.

"She Recognizes a Need—Not to Forget": the *Groyser Kundes* mirrors the public but especially Jewish mourning shortly after the calamity of New York's 1911 Triangle Fire. The caption reads, "Working Class: Where would they come from and who would they be? They are my victims. Oh, I recognize them, I recognize them!" The artist is Lola, aka Leon Israel.

זי דערקענט די „נים דעו וענעש ...

אַרבײטער קלאַס: — פֿון וואַנען זיי זאָלען ניט קומען און ווער זיי זאָלען ניט זיין, זיי זיינען מיינע קרבנות. אָ, איך דערקען זיי, איך דערקען זיי !...

דער גרױסער קונדס

דער מאַדערנער באַפֿרײַער

מיט דעם צױבער-שטעקען פֿון װיסענשאַפֿט װעט דער מאַדערנער נבֿיא שפּאַלטען דעם
ים על-דאַ-ס-כּיי און װעט דאָס אַרבײַטער-פֿאָלק אַריבערהֿרען אין אָרץ זבֿת חלב ודבֿש.
אין לאַנד פֿון עקאָנאָמישער פֿרײַהים.

MARX, THE WONDER-WORKER, LEADS THE CHILDREN OF ISRAEL THROUGH THE PERILS TO PARADISE

"The Modern Liberator": Karl Marx leads the (Jewish) children through the
Red Sea of woes. His caption reads, "With his magic staff of knowledge, the
modern prophet splits the sea and will lead the working class to the land of
milk and honey, the land of economic freedom." On his staff, "Knowledge";
on the sun, "Economic Freedom"; and on the waves of danger, "Child Labor,
Tenement Houses, Backroom Politics, Economic Depressions, Slack, War,
Prostitution, Hunger, Need, Slavery, Corruption and Rotten Food." The artist
is S. (Saul) Raskin in the *Groyser Kundes*, 1912.

פֿון אַ חזיר אַ האָר

פֿעטערסאָנער סטרײַקער

"A Hair from a Pig": Abraham Cahan, editor of the *Forward* newspaper, gives only nominal assistance to the 1913, IWW-led strike in Paterson, New Jersey. The avowed socialist Cahan is seen as a capitalist with the Forward building coming out of his hat and a bankbook in his hand. He says, "Here, take this and know that I have a socialist heart that bleeds for the hungry striker." To which the Paterson striker answers, "Yeah, it could be that you have a socialist heart, but it's covered by a capitalist bank-book." And to the side, he adds, "Well, a pig's hair is also good." The artist is Lola, aka Leon Israel, in the *Groyser Kundes*, 1913.

„פֿאָרווערטס": נאַ, און ווייס, אַז איך האָב אַ סאָציאַליסטישע האַרץ וואָס
בלוטעט פֿאַר דעם הונגעריגען סטרײַקער!

פֿעטערסאָנער סטרײַקער: יאָ, ס'קען זײַן, אַז דו האָסט אַ סאָציאַליסטישעס
האַרץ, אָבער דו האַלסט עס פֿערדעקט מיט אַ קאַפּיטאַליסטישען באַנק בוך. (אָן אַ
זײַט)! וועלל, פֿון אַ חזיר אַ האָר איז אויך גוט....

"Eser Makhes, or the Ten Plagues," with images going down in columns. The plagues include the Ku Klux Klan, labor bureaucrats, yellow journalism, apartment evictions, long hours, unemployment, police brutality, etc., all seen as the historical enemies of the Jews. The artist is Yosel Kutler, from *Boydek Khomets* (1934), a one-shot satirical magazine published in New York, aimed at orthodoxies of (almost) every Jewish and capitalist kind. Its appearance coincided with the high point after the 1890s of outright antireligious expression in the Jewish American Left. Afterward, amid the Popular Front and beyond, atheists were more cautious at causing offense.

"Striker" by William Gropper, with figures going right to left. A radical cartoonist and occasional oil painter, and hugely popular among Yiddish-speaking unionists, Gropper picked up the contemporary comics style for this narrative of working-class life. Published in *di Goldene Mideneh* (New York: Morgn Frayhayt, 1929), a volume produced by the Left Yiddish newspaper of record, the title is a bitter satire on the status of the United States as a "golden land" and savior of Jewishness.

"Gimpl Binish, the Matchmaker" by Samuel Zagat, from *di Varhayt*, 1918. Gimpl meets Max, a former client, on the street, and tells him how important the draft legislation is for the war effort: "You're not working and you're not fighting either." To which Max answers: "True, I'm not working, but on account of that, I'm fighting with my wife every day!"

"Gimpl Binish, the Matchmaker" by Zagat, from *di Varhayt*, December 24, 1914. Jewish children seek to celebrate "Santy Claus." After they find a tree, Gimpl curses little Notke and Motke: "Get out of here with your Gentile stuff, you brats! Christmas trees, I'll give you!" with a kick in the rears.

"Gimpl Binish, the Matchmaker" by Zagat, from *di Varhayt*,
March 12, 1915. This strip deals with high cost of owning a car.
Gimpl says, "Giddyap, horsie, I mean car!" The "fixer" offers
to fix it for ten bucks and Gimpl hands over the money. The
mechanic says, "Thanks! Now, just pour in some gasoline!"

"Gimpl Binish, the Matchmaker" by Zagat, from *di Varhayt*, May 18, 1916. Gimpl says, "Of course he can play ball, but look out for accidents!" A kid offers to play ball with Gimpl, and the matchmaker actually hits it right at a neighborhood cop. Watching him run, the cop runs after him, "He's too old to be a child, and too fast to be a German spy!"

"Moving Pictures": Zagat's comical take on the effect of silent film on children, from *di Varhayt*, 1912. After watching a kidnapping in a movie, children try it at home and get their comeuppance.

"Before and After the Wedding" by Zuni Maud, from *forverts*, December 10, 1916. *Before*, Zalman talks and fiancée Golda listens—everything is lovely: "We will treat each other like little doves!" *After*, she talks at him and he sits silently bored. And later on, she talks and talks while he jumps up and the neighbors listen! (She says, "You should rot like a dead creature and break down like a watch!")

"The Angel of Death Trust Company" by Maud, from *forverts*, February 25, 1916. Zishe, ravished with hunger, gets a meal with meat for twenty-six cents. Then he gets sick, goes to "an expert" who charges him and sends him to a doctor who charges him more and gives Zishe medicine that makes him sicker. In a little while he drops dead. His gravestone reads, "Zishe HaCohen, Born in Minsk, Died from Lunch." The "expert," the doctor, and the grave digger put up a few dollars—and go out to look for more customers.

"Charlie Howyadoin?": Zuni Maud's signature strip. His character Charlie tells his friend that he is looking for a job making knee pants. His friend responds that there's no work there now, to which Charlie responds, "I know, but I'm sick of being unemployed in the pocketbook industry!" From *di Tsayt*, 1921.

"Abie the Agent" by Harry Hershfield, 1914–1915, and
his character's domestic troubles while making a speech,
riding a train, and sitting for a portrait.

Now You Know How to Cut Your Own Hair

LAUGHING HYENA (A) LAUGHS - BLIND MOUSE (B) THINKS HYENA IS LAUGHING AT HIM, GETS INSULTED, WALKS OFF AND BUMPS INTO DISC (C) MOTION OF DISC IS TRANS- FERRED THROUGH SERIES OF RODS AND DISCS (D-E) TO STUFFED GLOVE (F), WHICH PUSHES WEAK, STARVING LILLIPUTIAN GOAT (G) AGAINST HEAD (H) - GOAT MOVES FORWARD AND EATS OFF HAIR UNTIL HE FALLS OVER INTO GOAT CRADLE (I) ON OTHER SIDE WHEN HE IS FULL.

N.B. ONE ORDINARY HEAD OF HAIR IS JUST ENOUGH TO FILL A REGULATION LILLIPUTIAN GOAT.

"Now You Know How to Cut Your Own Hair," by Rube Goldberg, a typical reflection on the silliness of modern society's obsession with progress. Reprinted by permission of Rube Goldberg, Inc.

HANDLE (A) OPENS DOOR (B) RELEASING SPECIAL-FORMULA LAXATIVE CATFOOD (C) DOWN CHUTE (D) AND INTO DISH (E), FROM WHICH KITTY-CAT (F) EATS. CAT'S TURDS (G) FALL WITH GREAT VELOCITY AND BOUNCE OFF UP-RAISED END OF SEE-SAW (H) WHICH CAUSES CANDLE (I) TO LIGHT CANNON (J). CANNONBALL (K) HAS SPREAD-SHOT OF SEDUCTIVE FEMALE MOUSE PAINTED ON IT. HORNY MALE MOUSE (L) RUNS TOWARD PICTURE ON HIS TREADMILL (M) WHICH RAISES AND LOWERS STRING (N) ATTACHED TO FLEA (O) WHO BITES SLEEPING DOG (P) ON TAIL. DOG CHASES HIS TAIL ROUND AND ROUND CAUSING CIRCULAR PLATFORM (Q) TO TURN PIPE (R) WHICH PULLS HANDLE (A) AND CAUSES ENTIRE PROCESS TO BEGIN ONE MORE TIME. PERSON (S) OBSERVING THIS DEVICE BECOMES DEPRESSED BY ITS USELESSNESS, AND REALIZES THE FUTILITY OF ALL EXISTENCE. HE GOES TO MEDICINE CABINET (T), TAKES OUT A BOTTLE OF SLEEPING PILLS (U) AND INGESTS A LETHAL OVERDOSE!

"Auto Destructo Suicide Device." Art Spiegelman's takeoff on Rube Goldberg, made more outrageous with dog poop and suicide, both presumably beyond Goldberg's permitted vistas. From *Shmate*, Summer 1983. Reprinted by permission of the artist.

DAVE'S DELICATESSEN (Appears in Colors in The Sunday Record)   By Milt Gross

Milt Gross, "Dave's Delicatessen," circa 1930.
One of Gross's many strips.

Milt Gross, "That's My Pop," 1936: a child's view of a
hopeless schnorrer or "good for nothing" of a father.

Milt Caniff's "Terry and the Pirates" at its antifascist apex, 1946. Reprinted by permission of the Caniff Estate.

Al Capp, "Li'l Abner," 1946. Reprinted by permission of the Capp Estate.

"Clifford": Jules Feiffer's own character, from the *Spirit* newspaper section, 1949. Reprinted in *Feiffer: The Collected Works, I*. Reprinted by permission of the artist.

"Feiffer" syndicated strip by Jules Feiffer, from the *Village Voice*,
February 18, 1965. Reprinted by permission of the artist.

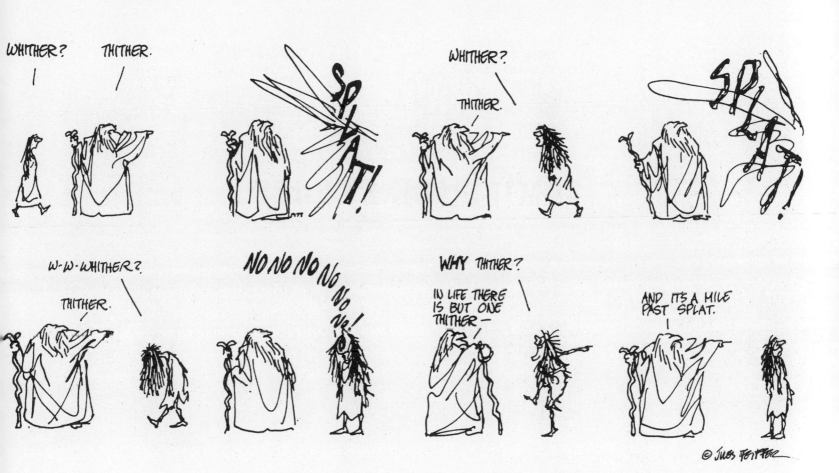

"Feiffer" syndicated strip by Jules Feiffer, from *Jules Feiffer's America: From Eisenhower to Reagan* (New York: Knopf, 1982). Reprinted by permission of the artist.

Chapter 2 **COMIC BOOK HEROES**

THE COMIC BOOK TRADE HAS ITS BACKSTORY IN GREATER NEW YORK'S rough-and-tumble *Yiddishe Gossen*, or "Jewish streets," of the 1910s, among the scrambling small-businessmen with mob pals and socialist relatives.[1] It was a milieu like none other, at least none other west of the Hudson River. Jewish gangsters would, of course, soon be practically everywhere the sun shone and big profits could be made, more powerful in distant and developing Arizona/Nevada than in old New York. But the pulp publishers were in New York, or not far beyond. The stamp has never quite left the product. Indeed, as we shall see, comics about Jewish gangsters in the early decades of immigration have become a source of interest and even an odd pride: this is Jewish American life revealed.

Meanwhile, Yiddish publishing—from religious books to the *Groyser Kundes* to the real big business of the *Daily Forward* and its rivals—offered a convenient entry point for Jews to break into the increasingly lucrative printing trade. By the 1920s, future comics giant Harry Donenfeld, stepson of an International Ladies' Garment Workers' Union organizer and active socialist, had figured out an angle in the English-language end of printing. When he began creating inserts with slick paper and two-color covers for the big Hearst magazines like *Cosmopolitan* and *Good Housekeeping*, he had an operation.

Donenfeld soon struck out on his own, notably in the sex end of the fast-rising pulp magazine trade. He is rumored to have been, sub rosa, the printer for Margaret Sanger's *Birth Control Review*, which risked post office prosecution by offering for sale contraceptive devices via mail order. By the 1920s, he was more likely to print titles like *Artists and Models*, with semi-nude portraits and titillating fiction. His own formal debut as a publisher came with *Juicy Tales* and *Hot Tales*, then *Spicy Detective Stories* (mixing in the increasingly popular crime theme), until he was indicted in 1934 for the showing of some pubic hair in *Pep*. By this time, Donenfeld needed a new career and adroitly moved toward a promising one.

According to an industry legend close enough to fact, it was another immigrant, salesman Max Ginsburg (under the last name "Gaines"), who, during the same years, invented the comic *book*. He approached the Eastern Color Printing Company and successfully proposed reprinting comic panels from newspapers and binding them in various forms to be given away as promotions for companies like Procter & Gamble. This move led to freestanding sales, with Gaines's own *Famous Funnies*, all of sixty-four pages and available for a dime in 1934, as a prototype for what followed: a stapled, four-color pulp booklet. Sold at first in the children's department of chain stores, *Famous Funnies* went like hotcakes. This was especially interesting to would-be entrepreneurs because the newspaper funny pages, like film cartoons, had been carefully designed for the whole family. *Famous Funnies* was still a reprint mechanism, but with it, comic books had nearly been born.

What comic books needed was a spectacular selling device, and eager entrepreneurs found in distant Cleveland a necessary protagonist, two younger-generation Jews too innocent to know a near-mobster if they saw one. They were not the wretched poor by any means in the heavily ethnic Glenville, one of those new neighborhoods where life in America looked pretty good, even for Jews. But they, too, were looking for the road upward.

The day that young Jerry Siegel's father was murdered in the family dry goods store, the boy's expectation of a dignified art school education faded out of sight. The shy lad who loved movies about muscular heroes began thinking of other paths to success. At the tender age of fourteen, he joined a rapidly expanding world of amateur writing and publishing known as fandom, and on his own typewriter, he produced a crude magazine, *Cosmic Stories*. He also joined the staff of the high school paper. He rose as late as possible before the school day and sometimes put his street clothes on over his pajamas, a habit that logically suggests a certain superhero motif.

Joe Shuster, born in Toronto (his cousin, part of the family that stayed behind, became half of the famed Canadian-based television comedy team of Wayne and Shuster), was to become the artist of the pair. A quiet bodybuilder who took the popular physical culture magazines of the day to heart (or limb), he found Siegel at the Glenville High *Torch*. After graduation, the two of them began turning out strips for the first wave of commercial comic experiments that failed to get newsstand distribution and lasted only a few issues. By 1936, when Franklin Roosevelt's reelection against Alf Landon stunned the pollsters but won the hearts of Jewish Americans with social programs, the two had most of the narrative for "the Super-man" in place.[2]

The alert Max Gaines promised to place what would soon become *Superman* in a new comics title but could not follow through. Gaines's collection of unpublished samples fell, however, into the hands of an adolescent staffer (and precocious comics artist) of the McClure syndicate, Sheldon Mayer. Mayer, a wonderful talent in his own right but best remembered as an editor, passed it on to the publishers of the new comic book *Action Comics*.[3] The two Clevelanders had meanwhile reconceptualized and redrawn the narrative and the art repeatedly, sensing real success after numerous unpromising efforts at other strips and more mundane heroes. It was 1938, and as the world trembled with war and rumors of war, newsstand readers went wild over the new comic. News dealers literally begged for more, sometimes selling more than 100 percent of the press run, thanks to reclaimed damaged copies.

Comics' success with the public had by this time grown wildly, none more so than *Superman*, by Schuster and Siegel, and *Batman*, drawn by Bob Kane and written by Bill Finger. They promised much for a pulp magazine industry always on the lookout for new audiences with money to spend, even as little as a dime. The comic book industry itself thus emerged, within two or three short years, as a new sweatshop industry of greater New York. Descendent of the original needles trade, comics largely reproduced the familiar Jewish story, including internal class conflict, but with a difference due mainly but not entirely to the miniature scale. A few key comics bosses never lost their own artistic aspirations, continuing to work with the factory hands, shaping and reshaping the evolving character of the product. The biggest bosses, meanwhile, remained the publishing corporations, set solidly in pulp magazine publication and distribution. During the relatively short span of comic books' golden age, no one would replace them.

By 1944, comics had become an almost unbelievable business, with an output of millions of units each month. Wartime had put money into so many hands—and GIs as well as male youngsters on the home front would buy practically anything visually entertaining—that the worst of the many competitive lines could hardly fail.[4] Harvey Kurtzman remarked in an interview he gave late in his life that the comic book industry was cursed by the power of its entrepreneurial founders, accountants with no vision and no interest in art. But they knew their business.[5]

The artists themselves, according to much anecdotal evidence, were personally inclined toward melancholy. A family background of Depression poverty, alienation in a field of distinctly limited possibilities, long hours, and highly repetitious tasks brought mental breakdowns, alcoholism, and similar symptoms. Many an artist aspired to a career in advertising. To accomplish this would have been almost literally selling out, but relatively few ever achieved the comfortable income that accompanied the big step into the higher circles of commercial hucksterism. This may help to account for the darkness in *Batman*, a nonintellectual or somewhat vulgarized but nevertheless effective expressionist take on the terrors of big-city life. It might also possibly account, in another mood, for the zestful escapism of comics featuring funny animals, among the most interesting of the trends evident early on, but one that grew increasingly weird with the proliferation of small comic companies and series toward the end of the war decade. Comics pitting mouse or bird against cat, or cat against human, almost all of them underdog heroes, were the heirs to the most imaginative cartoons' earlier years and more abundant than them—until television cut them down.

Realism had never been a major aspect of the comics narrative. But it was never altogether absent, and it took on a new life in comics with the grimness of the world setting and the appearance of film noir, dated by later critics to the release of *The Maltese Falcon* (1941). The heavily inflected sense of societal alienation that emerged around this time was shared by a most unique Irishman and comics packager, Lev Gleason. A small-fry publisher on his own since the late 1930s, Gleason had given most of his energy until 1940 to pulps, including the Popular Front–ish weekly named *Friday*, which was killed, overnight, by the announcement of the Hitler-Stalin Pact. In early 1941, as the story goes, Gleason learned that he could take millions of pages of newsprint on highly limited consignment—only if he could turn out a publishable comic book *over a weekend*. Luckily, he was already working with one of the most promising writer-editor-artists of the trade, Charles Biro, and a semideveloped superhero character, Daredevil. A team of furious postadolescent writers and artists was quickly pulled together, and *Daredevil* appeared as its own comic, with a ferocious hatred of Nazism still hardly expressed in the field. While the United States was still formally at peace and the Soviet Union had not yet been invaded, Daredevil personally punched out the lights of the Führer, inside a cover promising "DAREDEVIL deals the ACE of DEATH to the Mad Merchant of HATE!"[6]

Identifiably Jewish superheroes would not have been an option for wartime comics, and neither artists, writers, nor publishers seemed even to contemplate them. Only a strained argument could place a real Jewish superhero (or just plain hero) in wartime comics. But it was true enough that wimpy Steve Rogers, child of the Lower East Side, rejected by the army as 4-F material, meanwhile ascended into Captain America with the help of one Professor Reinstein (who is promptly murdered by a Nazi spy). "Cap" also regularly battered the Führer with punches. A child of his comic book time and place, Steve/Cap never actually stopped being the blond hero fighting against all manner of swarthy characters around the world.[7]

The team's next big venture, and their most original, *Crime Does Not Pay*, was launched in 1942. Advertisements announced it thus: "The most sensational comic idea ever is sweeping the country. Crime comics give you the real facts. . . ." Not precisely or entirely a comic book (anticipating later experiments with a mixture of photographs of criminals, gun molls, and corpses), it described itself as a "force for good in the community!" In these narratives, the police were not seen as a particularly effective or even admirable part of the struggle, and even the portraits of violent gangsters were for the most part rooted in backgrounds of slums and social injustice.

Rising out of such backgrounds, the criminals got their comeuppance on the final pages, before which they had enjoyed riches and notoriety.

Gleason and his staff, led by Biro, quickly repeated themselves in half a dozen titles, including the Dostoyevsky-inspired *Crime and Punishment*. In 1946, Gleason found himself in front of a congressional committee, accused of supporting the Spanish Republic years earlier and supporting America's Russian allies during the war. But this was only an early Cold War probe and he successfully got himself off the hook. *Crime Does Not Pay*, with hundreds of issues published under that rubric, remained the most successful of Gleason's titles, with an estimated (by himself, in probable exaggeration) print run of 5 million copies per issue. Comic imitators sprang into action, launching dozens of similar-sounding titles; none was nearly as successful, but there were enough of them to poison the well with ever greater degrees of psychopathic violence, thus encouraging would-be censors.[8]

Another enterprising publisher meanwhile found a way to combine uplift with steady sales. It was a marvel of the trade: Classics Illustrated. With editions in twenty-six languages and thirty-six countries, and a backlist that, unlike other comics, continued in large part to remain continuously in print, it was a grand success. Albert Lewis Kanter, son of Russian Jewish immigrants living in Nashua, New Hampshire, was the driving force behind it. A book salesman and the designer of a popular appointment diary for medical professionals, Kanter found himself almost by accident packaging remaindered comics.

There had been fitful experiments in serializing severely adapted classics into the funny papers and the first regular comic books, but nothing had struck gold. Kanter arranged financing, and in 1941 the first run of his new company appeared. *The Three Musketeers*, *Ivanhoe*, and *The Count of Monte Cristo* set a tone for hundreds of adaptations to follow. They carried no advertising—then a first in comic books—and used the space at the end for educational or patriotic material. It was clearly an appeal to educators and concerned parents, and it worked gloriously.[9]

The level of storytelling and artistic talent alike varied greatly at Classics and by no means always matched that of a title's source material. H.G. Wells's science fiction adventures were more likely to look like other science fiction genre comics, *Dr. Jekyll and Mr. Hyde* looked more like horror comics, and so on. More important than these influences was the job shop that took over actual production in 1945, owned by Will Eisner's erstwhile partner Jerry Iger, who employed some of the best talent in the business. Artists whose truest influences had been left-wing expressionists Lynd Ward and Rockwell Kent, or the rare African American artist, or artists so strange that their androgynous figures had special appeal (it was thought) to younger children, or would-be intellectuals who took pride in a comic version of *The Iliad*—these were all types whose work presumably appealed to Kanter's tastes or his salesman's instincts.

By the time Iger dropped the account in the 1950s, Classics had published the bulk of its 100 million copies and reached most of the 25,000 schools that used them as part of the curriculum. A comic adaptation of Shakespeare's *Julius Caesar*, reputedly rendered with the cooperation of the New York University staff, caught the attention of the *New York Times*— and of Frederic Wertham.

A German-Jewish émigré, co-author (with his wife) of a widely recognized textbook on the physiology of the brain, Wertham (originally Frederic J. Wertheimer) was president of the Association for the Advancement of Psychotherapy when he launched his portentous campaign. In another age, the charge of corrupting children's minds would likely have carried less weight. But the specter of "juvenile delinquency" hovered over the cityscapes of urban neighborhoods ravaged by superhighways and loaded with mostly new, impoverished populations of nonwhites. Simultaneously, the red scare moved into its highest phase, with House Un-American Activities Committee hearings carried out as a political circus employed to break strikes or wipe out left-wing unions and threaten Hollywood, radio, and television.[10]

Seizing his moment in the sun, Wertham appeared at hearings giving dramatic testimony, first in the New York state legislature and then in the Senate of the U.S. Congress. Perhaps the charge of promoting homosexuality (Batman and Robin seem to have been the guilty ones) came closest to other perceived threats—including the image of a calculating Jewish capitalist, a sentiment no longer acceptable in congressional hearings but very much alive in popular thought. Wertham's bombshell *Seduction of the Innocent* (1954) provided ballast to the case that he had been making in hearings, hitting comics—very much like the blacklisting attack on Hollywood—at a moment when economic conditions were so precarious as to induce panic and near collapse. For comics, unlike Hollywood, the blockbuster days were never to return, except as the basis for films and video games.[11]

This story also bears heavily upon one other operation, arguably the apex of comic realism as well as concentrated imaginative attention: EC Comics, some of whose finest artists came over to a reduced but determined Classics when EC dropped all its comics for *Mad* magazine. There hangs a tale that rests first upon a final appearance of Max Gaines, who died in 1947 in a boating accident. His son William M. Gaines, a college student indifferent to the comics business, suddenly found himself heir to a small and heavily indebted publishing empire.[12] Bill Gaines was the half-Jew as fighting liberal and, more than that, a nonartist of unexpected artistic vision. Some of his early titles read as semiconscious satires on the clichés of comics, such as *Moon Girl Fights Crime*. It should also be remembered that film, the closest art form to comics, was by this time undergoing subtle shifts often most noticeable in the B-movie genres, memorably in what would later be called film noir but also in genre satires by Abbott and Costello, among others, poking fun at horror movies, westerns, and so on. The young artists that Gaines attracted had the same mentality, a weariness of the hyped patriotism and, even more, the forced social order of the war years, and the sense that the evolving consumer society, with its underside of political and cultural witch hunts, was full of hypocrisies large and small. Will Elder and Harvey Kurtzman were talents as large as any the comics industry had seen, but they were talents of a particular kind that had never before existed.

The industry had never seen the likes of EC's "New Trend" comics, proudly launched in 1950. Not so different from the distinctly left-wing films of a few years earlier, made on small budgets by some of the finest talents in Hollywood, the New Trend comics blossomed in style and content for a brilliant few years before repression wiped them out. As in the case of the films, a mixture of darkness and dark humor hit the target and left an enduring memory behind.

The company started out with little prospect of credit when William Gaines took it over; only a combination of sure sellers and a product that induced extreme reader loyalty could lift the little EC, whose seldom-used formal title, Educational Comics, the younger Gaines changed to Entertaining Comics. Hiring Al Feldstein, a talented editor-artist his own age, Gaines set out a course of highly artistic melodramas. Based on radio suspense programs that had a touch of the ghastly, *The Crypt of Terror* and *The Vault of Horror* were distinctly grotesque, usually about wrongdoers whose sins and crime would not be punished by the law. They were such a hit that they prompted dozens of imitations overnight, and ultimately invited disaster.

Only a little less spectacular and unique was the social drama of *ShockSuspense* and *SuspenStories*. Very much the parallel of noir, with treacherous romantic pacts, betrayals, murders, and assorted crimes, they also included a portion of what Gaines referred to as "preachy" stories, generally attacking some element of popular prejudice, such as racism or lynch-mob pseudo-patriotism and the hypocrisy so familiar from the contemporary monologues of the FBI's J. Edgar Hoover. Crime comics had meanwhile become a drug on the market by 1950, mostly disappearing, and none of the competitors remotely undertook the mission that the progressive Gaines and his staff considered right and necessary.

But the greatest EC innovations lay just ahead. *Weird Science Fiction* and *Science Fiction Fantasy* might rightly be called an experiment in tragic realism—or perhaps surrealism. The booming pulp sci-fi trade, soon to take on new dimensions with the proliferation of paperbacks, was part bug-eyed monsters and extreme conservatism of the Robert Heinlein variety, looking for new extraterrestrial frontiers to conquer, and part downright liberalism, even vaguely radical, a reflection of the backgrounds of many of the writers and editors in Manhattan in the 1930s and of a tradition of naysayers who suspected fresh horrors in every government or industry claim of progress. Along with a few liberal filmmakers, it was heavily involved in the popular discussion of atomic or nuclear war and the doom of a self-proud civilization (or empire).[13]

Harvey Kurtzman, destined to be a towering figure of comic art, started out with many of his future collaborators in the Bronx at the new High School of Music and Art. Between high school and the army, he worked in the studio of illustrator Louis Ferstadt, who supplied comics to the *Daily Worker* when not occupied with commercial and studio work. After the war, working his way through the lower levels of the comics trade in the later 1940s, Kurtzman never quite lost his didactic streak. He was involved in (among other things) the educational effort to explain the dangers of syphilis, in a comic produced by Max Gaines's brother, before joining EC in 1950. Kurtzman pressed his case for nonfiction projects with Gaines and was handed the editorial responsibility (as well as most of the writing and a fair amount of the drawing) for two new war comic series, *Two-Fisted Tales* and *Frontline Combat*. War stories had been a staple of the trade since its beginning, swelling into a huge enterprise during the 1940s, and would remain so in comic revival after revival. But the war comics with the Kurtzman touch were distinctively, drastically different: they were most always antiwar, in affect if not in story line.[14]

First of all, these were undoubtedly the most thoroughly researched historical comics that had ever appeared on American newsstands. The stories ranged from Roman times and earlier, to the age of European conquerors at home and in the New World, to the American Revolution, the Civil War, and also the Native American wars, and through the U.S. invasion of Cuba in the Spanish-American War, the first and second World Wars, and Korea. Only perhaps the realist war novels by the likes of James Jones and Norman Mailer, and a small handful of daring films, could compare as popular, realistic entertainment.

Not all the details came from books. Kurtzman and his friends had themselves lived through the antifascist war, and servicemen who read EC comics eagerly supplied information that, the editors claimed, could not have been found elsewhere. Occasionally, Kurtzman and his artists even spoke from the viewpoint of enemy combatants and civilians. War was the real enemy, the look of dead and wounded soldiers as dreadful as anything in *The Vault of Horror*.

Among the talents that blossomed at EC, none of the nonsatirists looms quite so large as Bernard Krigstein.[15] Growing up as the son of immigrants in Brooklyn in the 1930s, he had a modestly successful businessman father who encouraged the boy's artistic aspirations. Attending Brooklyn College, the would-be artist fell in love with the daughter of a communist and Yiddishist. He joined the comics trade by accident and had only made a beginning when he was inducted into the army in 1943. Mustered out two years later, Krigstein once again found his living in comics. It took years of slogging through the lower end of the trade before he discovered a home at EC. Along the way, he became a tireless activist in the nearest thing to a union that the comic book artists ever could manage, the now-forgotten Society of Comic Book Illustrators. Comic publishers, in response, raised the salaries and bettered the work conditions of their favorite artists, letting others know that their talents were dispensable. The union effort collapsed.

By 1953, he was firmly established at EC and widely considered among fellow innovators as the finest of the nonhumor artists. His modernist panels preview all the best of today's graphic novel stylists, an adaptation of expressionism in a different medium. But it was through *Frontline Combat* and *Two-Fisted Tales*, EC's war comic lines, that Krigstein achieved his true status—with one exception: the story "Master Race," about a former Nazi war criminal spotted on the subway. Written by EC editor Al Feldstein, published in the soon-obscure *Impact Comics* in 1955, "Master Race" has remained for devotees Krigstein's signature piece, decisive proof of what he might have accomplished if given a little more of an opportunity.

Will Elder, Krigstein's match but in a different key, was a talent as large as Al Capp or Rube Goldberg, but his golden days were short. Born Wolf Eisenberg, he was set on his life's path when he attended the High School of Music and Art with Kurtzman and future satirical artist Al Jaffee. Home from the service, he worked in many comic genres and joined the EC crew in 1951. There he set his sense of humor loose, in *Mad*.

Gaines was looking for more work to pile on Kurtzman. Kurtzman appreciated the spirit of college humor magazines, which had been around since the 1920s but were armed with a new vigor with the return of the GIs in the late 1940s. He admired a failed comic magazine created by Charles Biro and the fearless college humor magazines flourishing among the ex-GIs. *Mad* started slowly, but Gaines covered the early losses, and soon it gained a fanatically loyal readership. Readers proudly enrolled themselves in the half-satirical Fan-Addict Club, a truly subversive and largely Jewish organization.

EC soon paid the price. An early issue of *Panic*, an in-house knockoff of *Mad*, was seized in Boston for ridiculing Santa Claus, while another issue led to the arrest of one of Gaines's assistants by the New York police. Gaines may have made a mistake in volunteering to testify at congressional hearings in 1954 without a cadre of fellow publishers; he believed that he could reason away the anxieties with sentiments that must have sounded like another form of treason to the Cold War politicians of the day. American children were by and large healthy of mind; it was the would-be censors who saw filth and perversion. Delinquency, consequently, was a social problem that could not be whisked away by censoring comics. "Our problems are economic and social and they are complex. Our people need understanding; they need to have affection, decent homes, decent food," he said in closing. It was pure New Dealism.[16]

The politicians were having none of it. The new Comics Code, written in part by the creators of Archie Comics, demanded servility. (EC had its revenge in small ways: a devastating satire, "Starchie," appeared in a 1955 issue of *Mad*, with Archie and Jughead as the real juvenile delinquents.) Days before the Comics Code took effect, Gaines put his horror and suspense comics on hold and placed his trust in Kurtzman's vision. What the artist-writer wanted was something strikingly new, so new that there were no real models for it. After a series of daunting developments, including Kurtzman's demand to have a controlling interest in the new magazine, the smoke cleared. Al Feldstein would be editor. Kurtzman and most of the artists, including Elder, were out of the picture.

From the first issue as a comic in 1952, *Mad* had an unmistakable Kurtzmanesque flavor, an almost indefinable take on popular culture as fascinating but also prone to corruption, including the endless cliché. By the third *Mad* issue and "Dragged Net" (signed by "Sergeant Elder"), *Mad* had hit the button. Elder's panels were filled with side jokes, like the mounted cop's head labeled "Mounted Police," the case of "selza" carried by safarigoers in the Congo, the sacks of kosher hams in a North Pole cave, and so on, endlessly. With or without Elder, Kurtzman could script a Lone Ranger whose gunshots just nicked criminals' trigger fingers, a Clark Kent who cleaned spittoons, and a disillusioned country girl who comes to town and learns to sell reefer to schoolchildren. The fifth issue carried an introduction by Gaines himself, shown with a halo, described as the son of "an International Communist Banker," a boy who grew up in a life of crime, stealing and selling dope, who then "took the cure . . . opened an establishment in a district of scarlet illumination . . . took the cure [again] . . . and finally, seeking the ultimate depravity and debasement, quite naturally turned to the comic book industry." His "Evil Comics" (apparently the true meaning of EC) were destined to be full of "sadism, snakes, masochism, pyromania, snakes, fetishes, snakes, necrophilia, phallic symbols and all that esoterica what I can't think of at the moment." In short, he and *Mad* were everything that Kanter of Classics Illustrated had sought to escape.

Mad, meanwhile, only continued to get madder for the next three years. In its October 1954 issue, shortly before its transformation into the magazine format, *Mad* announced that it was headed "underground," a word that during the mid-1950s still recalled wartime partisans fighting behind fascist lines. In one panel, a subversive-looking comic publisher is peddling comics on a street corner to a child, and in the next, the pseudo-documentation of a "comic book raid," we see a criminal-looking cartoonist and another with three eyes (i.e., an alien) "rounded up in their hide-out," all the imagined contemporary dangers rolled up into one.

There is not a single one of the "comix" artists of the 1960s–70s who did not read *Mad*, and few were unaware of Kurtzman's later, commercially failed magazines *Trump*, *Humbug*, and *Help!* and his long-running *Playboy* strip "Little Annie Fanny." *Help!* magazine (1960–65) happened to publish several of the key comix artists, as Kurtzman—the failing business exec—drew Crumb and Art Spiegelman under his creative wing. From a more strictly artistic-publication standpoint, he created something equally fascinating, if instantly obscure: *Harvey Kurtzman's Jungle Book* (1959), entirely drawn by Kurtzman.

Jungle Book featured a satire of small-town racist life in the South, which Kurtzman had seen up close while stationed there in the service. "Decadence Degenerated" also took on the short-term Hollywood phenomenon of novelistic adaptations, from William Faulkner to Tennessee Williams.[17] A notable piece on Freudianism ("A gripping tale of schizophrenia of the sage-brush and paranoia on the prairie") called "Compulsion on the Range" had a fresh Bronx angle on the West ("Someday people will realize that Indians . . . were the good guys and not the bad guys," says the good guy, to which his outlaw nemesis responds, "Yew talk lak a dang Bolsheviki"). A TV-detective satire of the phenomenally popular Peter Gunn, "Thelonious Violence," filled out much of the rest of the book. Kurtzman saved his greatest intensity, however, for one of the iconic popular culture novels/films of the fifties, *The Man in the Gray Flannel Suit*, restyling it as "The Organization Man in the Grey Flannel Executive Suite" and aiming it at the magazine industry where Kurtzman had suffered so badly. "Schlock Publications" was the world that Kurtzman knew best, and he may himself have easily been "this idiot," the young idealist who enters a career hoping to make a change in American intellectual and popular culture for the better. But here, the males are all bitter cynics and hacks, and the women are nubile secretaries destined to be pursued, pinched, and at last successfully propositioned. The steady corruption of our protagonist, the naïf Goodman Beaver, in the heart of business culture abusing both art and ideas forces him to become, in the end, everything that he had once despised. Thanks to a subsequent sex change, the same Goodman Beaver would become Little Annie Fanny, at once a badly needed source of Kurtzman family income and a source of artistic frustration for the rest of the creator's life.

The later praise for Kurtzman from Art Spiegelman and others, no few of them students in Kurtzman's comics course at the School of Visual Arts, was fervent. The genius editor was, however, fairly aghast at the developments from the mid-1960s onward and uncomprehending of the sheer wildness of underground comix. A child of the New Deal who had dreamed of a racially egalitarian society and did his best work exploring his own dread of the Cold War world, Kurtzman had never imagined long hair, Black Power, LSD, and women's, gay, or lesbian liberation as vehicles for challenging the system.

The final issue of *Mad* comics featured a cover with a single word framed in the center: "THINK." The rest of the issue wasn't terribly memorable, although the Okefenokee swamp of Gopo Gossom (aka Pogo Possum) was destroyed in a nuclear war—this in 1955, a year of atomic bomb public-safety drills and nonviolent resistance to the drills by peaceniks, notably in Manhattan. The future came suddenly when Gaines dropped his last efforts at comics ("picto-stories," black-and-white realist comics that were a market failure) for the single project of *Mad* magazine. It is notable that Albert Kanter, continuing Classics Illustrated, also resisted joining the Comics Code Authority, perhaps not only on a point of artistic integrity. EC star Joe Orlando's first book, *Caesar's Conquests*, happened to be adapted by a blacklisted former school principal, Annette Rubinstein, one of the real Jewish and Marxist literary figures of the age.[18]

That Classics struggled onward for a time (and has been succeeded in the twenty-first century, albeit indirectly, by a new line from a small

Midwestern publisher, Graphic Classics) was a tribute to the power of the idea. In much the same way that a small circle of mostly Jewish left-wing women found a niche in the growing market of young adult books exploring scientific topics, Classics kept its niche.[19] Roberta Strauss, a close friend of Isaac Bashevis Singer and a nonacademic nonfiction writer of real commitment (her post-comics-career books include *America's Reign of Terror: World War I, the Red Scare, and the Palmer Raids* and *Joe McCarthy and McCarthyism: The Hate That Haunts America*), had joined Classics in 1953, after graduating from Hunter College. As committed to historical accuracy as Harvey Kurtzman (and in that way, humor aside, his successor in the trade), Strauss oversaw the reissuing of many of the best titles. By the time of her departure in 1963, Classics was no longer issuing new titles in the United States, thanks to loss of distributors. Kanter himself moved to the United Kingdom, overseeing Classics' European production, which had outgrown its U.S. founders. A late moment of revival in the United States from 1967 to 1971, under a noted Catholic conservative businessman, nevertheless climaxed with *Negro Americans: The Early Years* as its final title. By that time, all the Classics plates had been sold and Kanter himself had passed. Several revival efforts have been made, none of them particularly successful.[20]

Another lonely if not lone voice was Jules Feiffer, whose extended comic novella *Munro*, later made into an award-winning animation feature in Prague by self-exiled director Gene Deitch, was a startling criticism of military life and the Korean War. Luckily, Feiffer landed at the new *Village Voice*, practically the only comics element among the most sophisticated antiestablishment journalism of the 1950s.[21] The freedom of the 1960s, with so much of the older print culture already beginning a process of slow fade, made that earlier accomplishment especially difficult to comprehend. When Roberta Strauss Feuerlicht died in 1991, her *New York Times* obit made no mention of her comics leadership, and that is all too characteristic of the way comic art remained virtually unobserved by critics.

From the mainstream comic industry point of view, things looked a great deal less bleak. The effect of the Comics Code, but also doubtless the continuing inroads made by television, flattened the market by the mid-1950s to half its former size, killing off the smaller companies. Marvel and DC raced back, if never to former sales figures then at least to hefty profits, with the reinvention of 1940s superheroes and the addition of new ones. The old masters (or hucksters) and their creations were definitely more postmodern. Jack Kirby (born Jacob Kurtzburg) was arguably the great purist of form, inventing and reinventing at the penciling phase, his inkers making many distinctions crucial to fans and later scholars alike. With awful dialogue and with Jewish references of any kind still absent until at least the mid-1960s, these superhero images had a genius quality all their own, at once expressionist and intentionally ironic, although devotees of non-comic art would likely think so. Comic book lines, like their stories, were once again being created by the newsprint ton and were only slightly more reflexive than they had been in their 1940s heyday.[22]

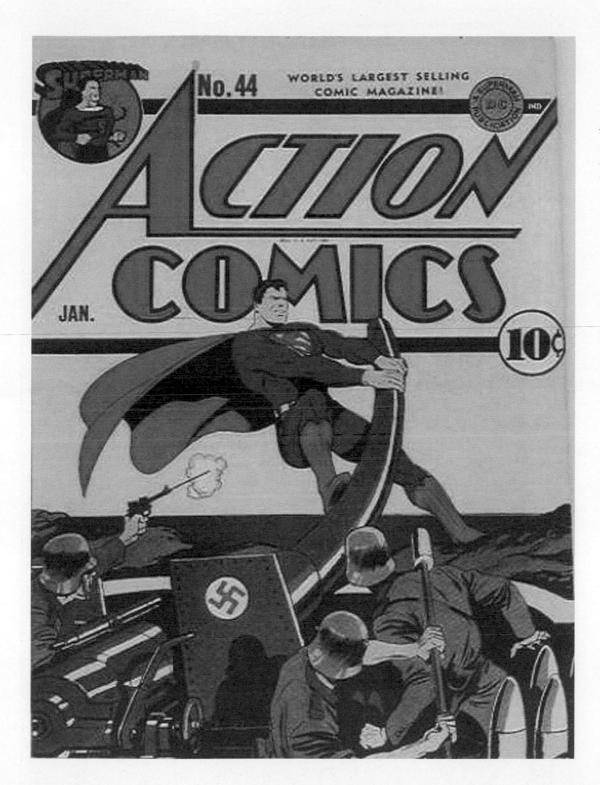

Action Comics, #44, 1943. Superman attacks a Nazi tank. Copyright DC Comics.

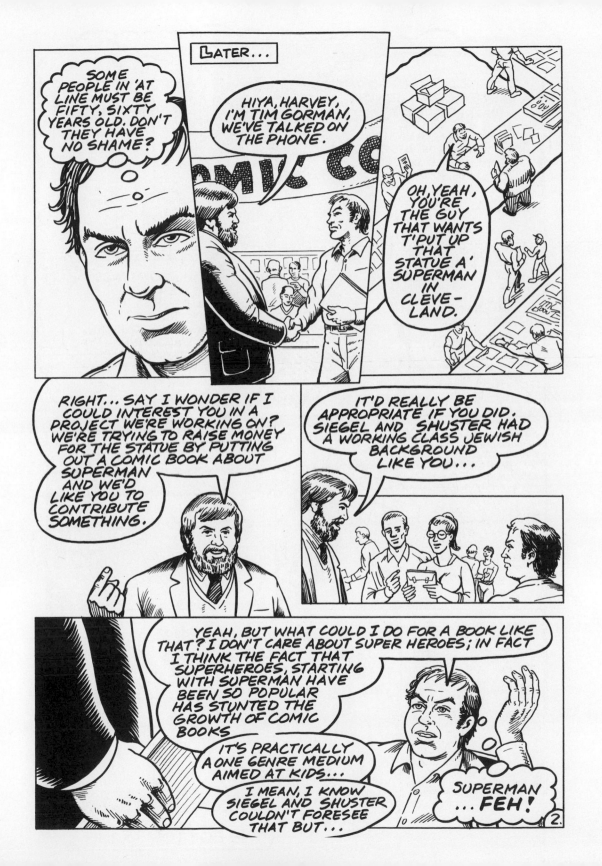

SOME PEOPLE IN 'AT LINE MUST BE FIFTY, SIXTY YEARS OLD. DON'T THEY HAVE NO SHAME?

LATER...

HIYA, HARVEY, I'M TIM GORMAN, WE'VE TALKED ON THE PHONE.

OH, YEAH, YOU'RE THE GUY THAT WANTS T'PUT UP THAT STATUE A' SUPERMAN IN CLEVELAND.

RIGHT... SAY I WONDER IF I COULD INTEREST YOU IN A PROJECT WE'RE WORKING ON? WE'RE TRYING TO RAISE MONEY FOR THE STATUE BY PUTTING OUT A COMIC BOOK ABOUT SUPERMAN AND WE'D LIKE YOU TO CONTRIBUTE SOMETHING.

IT'D REALLY BE APPROPRIATE IF YOU DID. SIEGEL AND SHUSTER HAD A WORKING CLASS JEWISH BACKGROUND LIKE YOU...

YEAH, BUT WHAT COULD I DO FOR A BOOK LIKE THAT? I DON'T CARE ABOUT SUPER HEROES; IN FACT I THINK THE FACT THAT SUPERHEROES, STARTING WITH SUPERMAN HAVE BEEN SO POPULAR HAS STUNTED THE GROWTH OF COMIC BOOKS

IT'S PRACTICALLY A ONE GENRE MEDIUM AIMED AT KIDS...

I MEAN, I KNOW SIEGEL AND SHUSTER COULDN'T FORESEE THAT BUT...

SUPERMAN ...FEH!

71

Detective Comics #27, 1939, the introduction of Batman. Copyright DC Comics.

"Scribbly and the Red Tornado" by Sheldon Mayer, from *All-American Comics*, 1941. Copyright DC Comics.

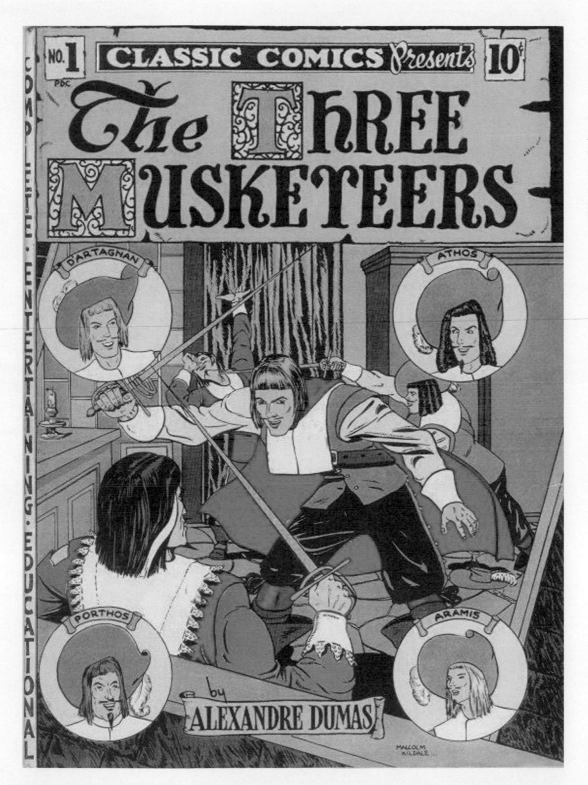

Cover of *The Three Musketeers*, Classics Comics (aka Classics Illustrated), 1941. Reprinted by permission of Jack Lake Productions, Inc.

"Art" cover,
Mad #22
(April 1955).
Collage by
Will Elder.
Copyright DC
Comics.

❶

MASTER ✠ RACE

YOU CAN **NEVER FORGET**, CAN YOU, CARL REISSMAN? EVEN **HERE**...IN **AMERICA**...TEN YEARS AND THOUSANDS OF MILES AWAY FROM YOUR NATIVE GERMANY... YOU CAN NEVER FORGET THOSE **BLOODY WAR YEARS**. THOSE MEMORIES WILL HAUNT YOU FOREVER...AS EVEN NOW THEY HAUNT YOU WHILE YOU DESCEND THE SUBWAY STAIRS INTO THE QUIET SEMI-DARKNESS...

YOUR ACCENT IS STILL THICK ALTHOUGH YOU HAVE MASTERED THE LANGUAGE OF YOUR NEW COUNTRY THAT TOOK YOU IN WITH OPEN ARMS WHEN YOU FINALLY ESCAPED FROM BELSEN CONCENTRATION CAMP. YOU SLIDE THE BILL UNDER THE BARRED CHANGE-BOOTH WINDOW...

TWO TOKENS, PLEASE.

YOU MOVE TO THE BUSY CLICKING TURNSTILES...SLIP THE SHINY TOKEN INTO THE THIN SLOT...AND PUSH THROUGH...

THE TRAIN ROARS OUT OF THE BLACK CAVERN, SHATTERING THE SILENCE OF THE ALMOST DESERTED STATION...

YOU STARE AT THE ONRUSHING STEEL MONSTER...

YOU BLINK AS THE FIRST CAR RUSHES BY AND ILLUMINATED WINDOWS FLASH IN AN EVER-SLOWING RHYTHM...

NO ONE COULD STOP THE BOOKS
FROM BEING BURNED...

"Twenty-Win"
written by Harvey
Kurtzman and
drawn by Will
Elder, *Humbug*,
1958.

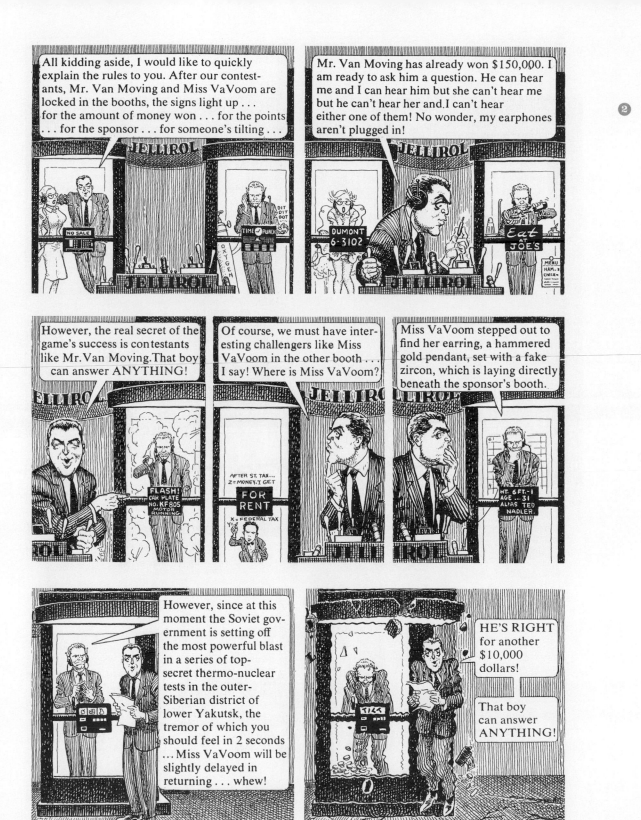

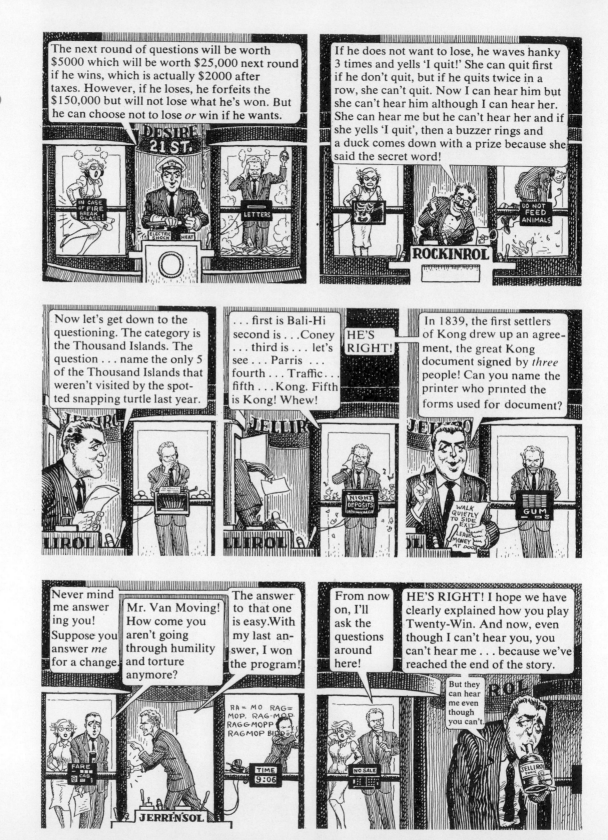

"Decadence Degenerated," a page from *Harvey Kurtzman's Jungle Book* (New York: Ballantine, 1959; reprinted by Kitchen Sink Press, 1988). Reprinted by permission of the Kurtzman Estate.

"Little Kimbo in Pinkoland" by Kim Deitch. Reprinted from *RAW* magazine (1991) by permission of the artist.

Chapter 3 **THE UNDERGROUND ERA**

THE SAGA OF "UNDERGROUND" CULTURE—FROM THE SUMMER OF Love to the spread of marijuana and peace insignias to GIs in Vietnam with the Black Power "dap" handshake—remains one of the great, complicated mixtures of events and mythology in the twentieth century. For comic artists, this was an extended moment of reinvention, from the margins inward, so much so that we can hardly imagine the comics of today without the surge of the late 1960s and 1970s.

The spiritual debt of counterculture artists to the overwhelmingly Jewish Beat generation has been emphasized repeatedly. There are many subtle undercurrents and overlaps binding Beat hipster culture to its generational successor, above all the Bay Area location itself. The counterculture artists who were most rebellious, famous, and notorious for flaunting all previous censorship aimed at comic art had followed Lenny Bruce (but also Allen Ginsberg) from deepest Gentile America into one of the most multicultural centers of the nation.[1] They gathered in Berkeley (destined to become more proportionally Jewish than Brooklyn, but not for decades yet), where, along with San Francisco's warehouse district, underground publishers physically set up shop. And they put themselves upon an artistic path no one had anticipated. Consciously and unconsciously, Jew and Gentile alike also recuperated varieties of Jewishness for their own purposes, creating a Jewish ambience that comic books and comics in the daily press had never possessed. As rebels of a particular kind, they could hardly do otherwise.

Strip for strip, character for character, underground comix reached many times more readers through (unpaid) reprints in the dozens of publications of the underground press than via individually printed books, although for a time the latter often had runs of ten to twenty thousand copies. By the early 1970s, a Robert Crumb solo book or Crumb-heavy anthology might reach a couple hundred thousand readers; the appearance of his work on the cover of a *New York Times Magazine* in 1972 was a kind of proof that the new art was going to leave a lasting impression, and not only on comic art. That King Crumb had meanwhile entered a "Jewish period" as vivid as Picasso's blue period could not be entirely a coincidence.

These young artists belonged to a different America way beyond Greater New York, the center of the nation's literate culture and the real homeland of American Jewishness. The underground newspapers feeding the market for a new kind of comic sprung up in newly hip zones like Austin, Texas, and Madison, Wisconsin, along with Greenwich Village and the East Village. Sometimes the counterculture cut a swath through a great city—like Los Angeles, New Orleans, and Chicago, among others—but mostly it was a near-campus phenomenon. Its publications can accurately be seen as the stepchildren of the earlier campus satire magazines that had set Kurtzman thinking about the creation of a satire magazine of a different kind way back in 1950. Its readership, constantly shifting, must have contained a smaller proportion of Jews, but as in the political movements on campus, Jewish voices were almost never absent. They were certainly present among the local lawyers defending the papers against censorship and police harassment, and among friendly professors who would write a check now and then.[2]

The marvel of it all is that suddenly, almost anything seemed possible for the contents of the comic art form—even a change of name, for "comix" became the favored term. From the beginning, the politics were radical and anticapitalist, at least in the vague hippie fashion, and were often more directly against the U.S. role in the world, as an extension of the U.S. occupation of Vietnam. The use of dope in various forms, mostly marijuana and LSD, was not far behind as a theme. Sex was also never long absent: more than anything else, nudity and outright sexual acts proved that the barriers put up against comic art in past generations were coming down fast.

The memory of censorship and downright repression nevertheless loomed large, larger, presumably, than it is ever likely to again. It is often forgotten how close in time and consciousness comic artists of the late 1960s were to the imposition of the Comics Code and the congressional hearings. A great deal of the comix's gratuitous sex and violence, or perhaps the rationalization of it within the artists' community—especially but not only with regard to female characters—could be ascribed to flaunting the break from all restrictions. Another part had to do with the support of the war by so much of the "straight" population. By the early 1970s, Last Gasp Eco-Funnies' *Slow Death* series took over the legacy of the EC horror comics of twenty years earlier.[3]

Why exactly did the creative and print center form on the West Coast? The first tabloids devoted to the comix were based on the East Coast, in Philadelphia (for a moment, with *Yarrowstalks*) and Greenwich Village (for a longer moment, with the *East Village Other*'s supplement *Gothic Blimp*, whose key artists would decamp westward). But the Left Coast was the real place for vernacular avant-gardes. One of the most widely read and influential of the underground newspapers boasting comix contents, the *Los Angeles Free Press*, founded in 1965 and edited by Art Kunkin, was connected loosely with a group of music clubs run by middle-aged Jewish businessmen rooted in the milieux of the region's multiracial political Left. Up north, Bill Graham, Holocaust survivor and linchpin of the Fillmore Auditorium rock concerts (he had previously been a publicity agent for the San Francisco Mime Troupe, founded and led in those years by Ronnie Davis, scion of a Jewish Bay Area beer brewer), set the entire underground comix phenomenon into motion by arranging for future undergrounders to do rock concert posters and for a particular young artist to draw one album cover illustration.[4] That artist was Robert Crumb and the drawing was for Big Brother and the Holding Company, aka Janis Joplin's group.[5] Poster stores became comix stores and/or comix publishers, and the artists had the kind of outlet that no comic artist or artist of any kind could have had earlier.

Underground comix, despite their limited lifespan, can be seen in retrospect to have deftly united the comic book form with the multiform rebelliousness in the air, adding a reflective commentary upon the basics of American culture, very much including the physical comic book form. Crumb brilliantly recuperated the look and feel of comic art, the vernacular street sensibility. The nostalgia for the particular vernacular that Woody Allen deployed ten and twenty years later was here already in Crumb's work, as were comic history and a generalized ethnicity (aging mothers and fathers looking not-quite-Americanized) pointing toward a kind of street-corner Jewishness.

Art Spiegelman was to observe later about his own work that his great early obstacle was the need to become "cartoony," situated artistically in the world of the vernacular of the 1910s–40s. It took years of close attention and laborious effort. Self-taught, hacking out greeting-card illustrations for a living, Crumb claimed to have reached a similar point through pure instinct, driven eons further into newly familiar territory by taking LSD when recovering memories of the comic art that kept him going while his family disintegrated and his military father bestowed mean slaps and meaner insults on his insufficiently virile artiste sons.

Was there anything really Jewish about this particular hypervernacular, collective backward look? It would be difficult to find anything in the artists' intent. And yet there are innumerable points of connection, some identified with New York lower-class affect or the Jewishness of the entertainment world, or a thousand other related subjects among the concentric circles of friends across the Bay Area who for a decade or more did exciting work on the printed page. For them, Jew and Gentile alike, the referencing was almost constant.

For starters, and not only because of Harvey Kurtzman, there was *Mad*. Why had its impact remained undiluted by the passing of years in those who had read it when they were, say, ten years old? Crumb has commented more than once that he has spent his working life striving to reach the *Mad* comics' intensity, without expectation of success. "Do I still feel like I'm trying to attain the kind of cohesive intensity achieved by the early Kurtzman *Mad* comics?" Crumb asked rhetorically in 1977, in response to my exceedingly pointed questions. "Is it still an unrealized dream of mine? The answer is . . . naturally . . . I think that's the 'culture' works," with artists like himself reaching toward the icons of their childhood.[6]

For that matter, the 1955 "Art" issue of *Mad*, satirizing abstract expressionism, could easily be seen as the original for the postmodern transpositions of images from the art world by Art Spiegelman as he reached the height of his powers in the mid-1970s. The most contentious legal issues of the underground turned out not to be sex after all, but satire—of Walt Disney's characters. The Air Pirates group's extensions of Mickey Mouse and other Disney characters added new dimensions to, but inevitably played upon, "Mickey Rodent," of *Mad* comics fame. Jewish artist Bobby London was among the little group that went to the mat with the eight-hundred-pound corporate gorilla. They could not win but they surely put up a fight.[7]

One might argue that the intensity of the sex in underground comix followed other Jewish preoccupations, updated from "spicy" pulps to Al Goldstein's notorious *Screw*, as much as they did the Tijuana bibles. A great number of older comic artists, male and female alike, had long wanted to work with a sexual content hitherto forbidden, and a portion of their most scintillating work had toyed with the near-forbidden, featuring scanty clothes and double-entendre conversation.

Trina Robbins was to complain, in later years, that the overdose of sexist sex, including violence and rape, from the late 1960s through the early 1970s had killed the comix by poisoning the well with revolting images. She exaggerated the effects, because so much of the underground proved transitory, while market-driven, scarcely artful soft porn would successfully capture a goodly chunk of the alternative comics business for a couple decades. But she was right in suggesting that some of the most promising developments were cut off, for a variety of reasons, from a wider audience. Robbins's own leading role in creating the feminist comic *It Ain't Me Babe* in 1970, followed by a dozen issues of *Wimmen's Comix* running well into the 1980s and a single over-the-top issue of *Wet Satin*, was notable and remains notable, among other reasons because female eros posed another direction for comics and gave encouragement to other artistic expressions.[8] Sadly, the promising if small genre of gay and lesbian comix had barely gotten under way when the comix crashed.

Robert Crumb's sexual obsessions operated strangely in the beginnings of the identity era, when "black is beautiful" incited a wider impulse toward what would be called body acceptance—and something beyond. The erotic identification of just those things that Jewish women had sought to expunge from their body image, most of them notably shared with African American women, made Crumb's cravings woman-positive despite the downsides. Considerable posteriors above (or rather, below) all, large and powerful hips, un-WASPy noses, and bushy hair stood out among a virtual catalog of fleshiness on display here. In *Motor City Comics* (1969), one of his first solo books, Crumb invented an urban guerrilla leader, Lenore Goldberg, whose Girl Commandos invade a meeting of high-ranking city bureaucrats and declare women liberated. Assaulted by the cops, Lenore escapes back to her apartment and to exuberant oral sex with her lover, boy (and seemingly goy) revolutionary Projunior. Satirical and lustfully admiring, Crumb had created a classic pursuit of otherness for American Jews. Of course, Crumb-haters wouldn't see it like that.

That same heroic year of 1969, in his similarly solo work *Big Ass Comix*, Crumb introduced "Dale Steinberger: The Jewish Cowgirl," adding, "She's nobody's Yiddisha mama, that's for sure," and in a small box, asking the readers, perhaps also himself, "What is this strange fascination with Jewish girls??" In Crumb's notebooks of the next several years, the erotic Jewess is, in the most realistic drawings of Crumb's portfolio, more or less Aline Kominsky (he claims to have invented the underage Honey Bunch Kominsky before meeting Aline, an extremely odd coincidence). His longtime artistic collaborator, second wife, and fellow exile in the south of France, Aline would be mother to future comic artist Sophie. Crumb had also entered, through Aline, the extended Jewish family, or *mishpokah*, with the broken-English-speaking immigrant grandparents living in Florida, and will ponder for the rest of his artistic life the tradition that he had entered through *Mad*, Lenny Bruce, and other fascinations of childhood at his first signs of being "different" so much earlier in life.

Aline Kominsky-Crumb was also, of course, her own story. A Long Island escapee and art school dropout, she found Crumb amidst his cycle of girlfriends, ex-wife, and assorted troubles. Her *Bunch Comix* (1980) is either high or low in generational sex exploration, depending naturally upon the eye of the beholder. "Blabette and Arnie" offers the painful saga of the dysfunctional suburban Jewish family in the postwar era. Based financially on the promise of schlock salesmanship, it looks like *Death of a Salesman*, and Arnie is indeed pretty soon discouraged by failure and then dead from cancer. The kids grow up borderline psychotics, Aline's stand-in escaping to art school and to promiscuity. These identity comics were among the most scathing views of Jewish suburban life imaginable, but her art was always certain to be contrasted with the incomparable Crumb's. She lost interest and drew less and less, but notably collaborated on pieces for the *New Yorker*, always near-cinema-verité work depicting fashion shopping and heavy drinking. *Need More Love* (2007) recuperated large chunks of her life, through prose and comics, as an elaborate diary, perhaps the largest statement of redemption through art that never quite believes in itself.

The other Jewish artists of the underground, until at least the mid-1970s, could be counted on the fingers of a hand. Kim Deitch, whose work has taken on a second life in the last few years, was there at the New York end of the birth of underground comix. He happened to be the only descendant, among the underground circles, of any noted artist—in Deitch's case of a famous and decidedly left-wing animator. His father, Gene Deitch, a comic illustrator for the *Record Changer*, a jazz magazine of the late 1940s, worked later at several animation studios, including as a director in the Mighty Mouse domain of Terrytoons, and invented the kid antihero Tom Terrific for *Captain Kangeroo*—until, mightily frustrated, he left for Prague and his own low-cost animation studio, thirty years before the collapse of the Eastern Bloc.

Gene Deitch taught his son a great deal about visual narrative techniques, but by Kim's account, *Mad* comics remained decisive.[9] He dropped out of the Pratt Institute, unable to fit himself into art school formalities; shipped out to sea Melville-style; and worked odd jobs, including a crucial stint as psychiatric aide in a White Plains hospital with an intact 1930s ambience. Best known for his time travels through the dreams and hitherto suppressed memories of marvelous characters, Deitch is, like Crumb, forever fascinated (or obsessed) with the vernacular creations of the 1910s–30s, especially in the demimonde of B entertainment like the circus and carnival.[10]

In the small but wildly creative circle of comic artists, Deitch's wife for a few years was none other than Trina Robbins. Daughter of a noted left-wing Yiddish journalist, she grew up an ardent comics fan, scarcely Jewish in any recognizable sense but deeply political. After relocating westward and separating from Deitch with their daughter, she would, in an artistic sense, self-consciously recuperate the various "girl comics" of her 1940s youth, from *Wonder Woman* and *Sheena, Queen of the Jungle* to teen fashion vehicles. Some of her own most charming material remained the reworking of comic book genres, and in later years she abandoned her drawing board to become a scripter. Her projects in women's history made her the erudite scholar-without-degree of American women cartoon and comic book artists.

None of the other Jewish women artists were quite so prolific as editor-artists, but Sharon Rudahl was certainly the most thoroughly steeped in Jewish lore and a definitely Jewish leftism. From her earliest published drawings, Rudahl's narrative reflected her own odyssey from teen years, early romance, and failed marriage to her craving for sexual and artistic liberation, which her family couldn't grasp. She reached an art and politics that seemed, at once, underappreciated for its special Jewish gender qualities and utterly natural, as if her grandmother, from Russia to Los Angeles, had offered her a model all along. Not surprisingly, she turned to the most exquisite treatments of Jewish sagas: the risings against the czar, the struggles of Lower East Side unionists, and the sense of connectedness with older left-wing Jewish generations. Nowhere else in the world of comics did these themes come alive so vividly, and it is no surprise that Rudahl hit her high point with a graphic biography of the great anarchist Emma Goldman. She had herself been, after all, Goldmanesque from the beginning of her experiments with art, sexuality, and her personal development.[11]

The crisis of comix arrived only a few years after that of the host underground press (the institutional survivors restyled themselves "alternative"). The "head shops" that provided comix with their over-the-counter outlets and represented unrespectable commerce generally, from bongs to blacklight and radical posters, were closing down thanks to new ordinances and rising storefront costs. The familiar combination of sex, dope, and antiestablishment humor had lost its aura of rebellion as coke parties, middleclass promiscuity, and the cynics of the *National Lampoon* took (over) the stage. To launch an unfamiliar art form in comic book format was by the mid-1970s a loner's project.[12]

Harvey Pekar's *American Splendor* was also, from its earliest issues, profoundly about memories of urban popular life in Cleveland, in these years mostly the hidden life of ethnic neighborhoods, flea markets, and resale shops, with ample references to kielbasa and Yiddishisms. Decades-past strikes where company thugs and police attacked strikers with heavy violence, aging memories of girlfriends (or near-girlfriends) mixed with the tales of their second-generation families, nostalgia tales told about Eleanor Roosevelt—all these memories led one way or another back to the teller, Pekar himself. It was, after all, *his* Cleveland, in some sense all an extension of his own family turf. And it was the connection of the Jewish with the vernacular, the Jewish American past, extending, through Pekar himself and the old-timers he encounters, into the present.[13] Crumb's crucial role in encouraging Pekar, himself drawing many of the most interesting pages of early *American Splendor*, was a kind of coming together of the underground with the Jewish past, just as both seemed in danger of being forgotten. Like film director Barry Levinson's Baltimore, this was a memory far away from the main dramatic scenes of American *Yiddishkayt*. But Cleveland, of course, is vivid in its own particular blue-collar way, which Pekar and his artists have explored unforgettably.

The short-lived anthological project *Arcade*, a totem of the time and place of underground comix creation, has no film or literary monument to prevent its disappearance from historical memory (unlike Pekar's *American Splendor*). Edited by Art Spiegelman and Bill Griffith, it sought to consolidate artistically and historically the crew of artists retreating from the collapse of underground comix.[14] *Arcade* was intended to move the project one step further, adopting an explanatory purpose about the inner history of popular culture, framed with a necessary (and, at least from some angles, necessarily Jewish) irony about the whole effort.

The new venture took shape, in spring 1975, as no comics anthology ever had or would (up to the present) again. Brandishing a Crumb cover—a more than full-bodied young Jewish woman oblivious to the funny animal creatures around her—and a collaboration of Spiegelman and Griffith in a comic "editorial" alongside the old-fashioned column of insider chatter, it featured Spiegelman's heavily Freudian "Cracking Jokes: A Brief Inquiry into Various Aspects of Humor." A regular feature, "Arcade Archives," reprinted the editor's favorite old-time comics and was in a sense a continuation of *Help!*—Kurtzman's final magazine that recalled from obscurity a few pages of slightly risqué World War II strips by Milt Caniff but could not, of course, have excerpted the Tijuana bibles as *Arcade* did, throwing censorship right out the window.

The premiere issue climaxed with Justin Green's version of Shakespere's *The Winter's Tale*, with Leontes played by the familiar Jewish Uncle Sol character from Green's narratives about the entertainment biz. Green, the antic artist-interpreter of popular culture history, was yet another Jewish adapter. Raised in suburban Chicago in a mixed marriage with a Gentile mother, Green first discovered the weirdo in himself—and perhaps fled to comics, as Crumb did, to escape fatherly slaps—when the family moved to Skokie, Illinois, home of upwardly mobile Jews. Green's private religious obsessions turned Catholic, but the jokes stayed Jewish.[15] Only in the pages of *Arcade* could he bring back Sgt. Bilko in a sixteenth-century commedia dell'arte. Had *Arcade* succeeded, it might also have succeeded in lifting up comic art to the level of serious acceptance still barely achieved by the end of the century. Co-editor Spiegelman remarked to an interviewer for the *Comics Journal*, some years later, that *Arcade* might have been the life raft on the sinking ship of the underground comix scene.[16] It didn't float. But it remained a signal effort in a certain direction.

The next artistic step was taken in the following decade. *Raw* magazine (1980–91), the brainchild of Art Spiegelman and his wife, the French artist (and future arts editor of the *New Yorker*) Françoise Mouly, might have worked commercially in various parts of Europe. Dedicated to the proposition that comics could be art, its launch followed a period of self-reflection in Spiegelman, a self-conscious recuperation of Jewish traditions, that is better discussed in the next chapter. But crucially, *Raw* (whose subtitle regularly changed but perhaps best captured the magazine's ethos in a 1989 edition: "High Culture for Lowbrows") drew heavily on non-U.S. artists, especially but not only Europeans. Comix artists would say that they had been thrown overboard for a combination of non-U.S. artists (mainly European and Asian) and former students of the School of Visual Arts. One might say the avant-garde returned to its essential character: New York and Elsewhere, far from a philistine America. Or more simply, it had ceased to be Californian.

Nothing like *Raw* had ever existed. In its pages, nonsequential narratives; non-narratives; sheer primitivism; lavish colored prints of sketchbooks; the early appearance of assorted young artists, including Drew Friedman and his images of Hollywood has-been stories—all could be seen as if they belonged together. The Bay Area underground, deeply rooted in U.S. comic book and funny paper traditions, all but disappeared here.

The tragedy was that the underground had been cut off in the most promising moment of its development, as surely as the *Masses* artists of the 1910s were when faced with jail and literary suppression. That earlier handful of rebellious artists mostly found their way professionally, thanks in no small part to a friendly left-liberal gallery culture. The large majority of underground artists, by contrast, stopped drawing, or at least stopped publishing, only a decade after their emergence. A very few publishers, Kurtzman devotee Denis Kitchen most prominently, struggled to keep things going and sought assorted means to fit a number of the underground artists into the comic-collectors or comic-fan circuit, bridging the gap to the 1990s generation of young artists and beyond, meanwhile reprinting collections of the greats (Al Capp, Will Eisner, Mort Caniff, and Kurtzman himself among them). The losses, nevertheless, were staggering.[17]

Afterward, and conspicuously in *Raw*, the actor-oriented and event-oriented comic images that had dominated the field since the rise of the funny pages were increasingly displaced or replaced by the authorial voice. Comic art thus arguably escaped its original medium, not necessarily a happy development to familiar readers of comics, but one very much on the mind of the youngest generations. Hereafter, at least in theory, the master could dominate the comic panel, as precursors of other kinds had dominated the canvas, the sculpture, and the cinematic statement.[18]

Comic art was now truly coming into its own.

"Dale Steinberger, The Jewish Cowgirl" by R. Crumb from *Big Ass Comix* #1 (San Francisco: RipOff Press, 1969). Reprinted by permission of the artist.

From *Motor City Comics* #1 by R. Crumb (San Francisco: RipOff Press, 1969). Reprinted by permission of the artist.

"Mein Rue Platz" by Sharon Rudahl, from Wimmen's Comix #5 (San Francisco: RipOff Press, 1983). Reprinted by permission of the artist.

"Let's have a little talk" by R. Crumb and Aline Kominsky. Reprinted from *Dirty Laundry* (1977) by permission of the artists.

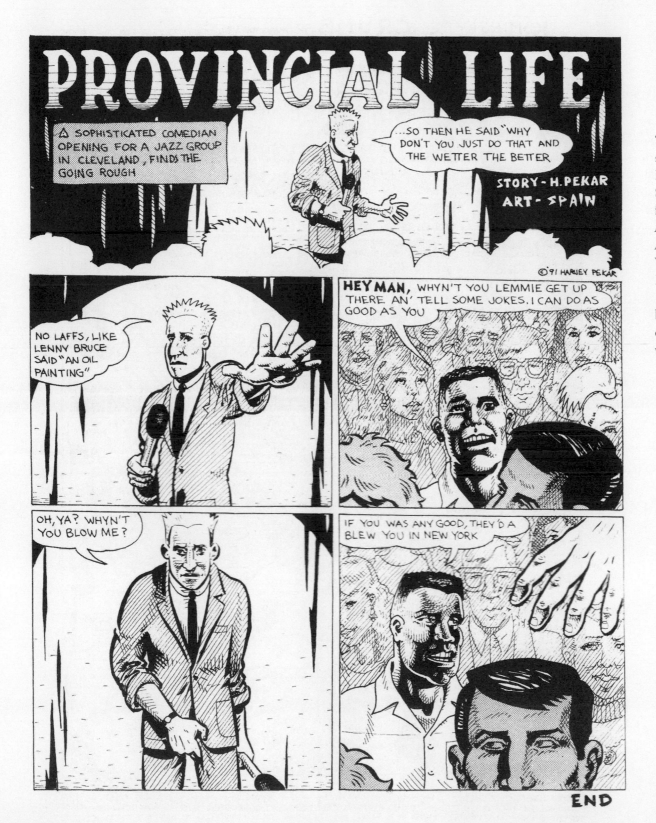

"Provincial Life" scripted by Harvey Pekar, drawn by Spain Rodriguez, from *The New American Splendor Anthology* (New York: Thunder's Mouth Press, 1993). Reprinted by permission of the artist and writer.

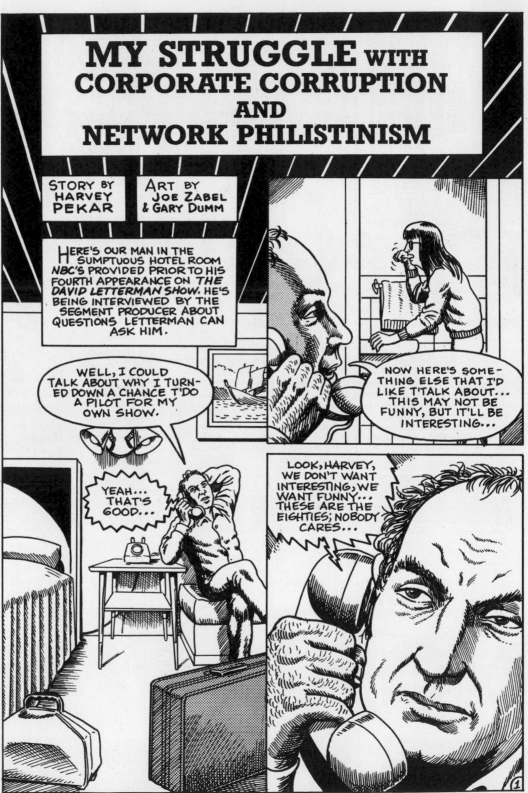

ON THE WAY OVER TO DO THE SHOW WITH FRIENDS WHO'LL BE IN THE AUDIENCE

WHAT'RE YOU GONNA TALK ABOUT?

I GOTTA TALK ABOUT G.E. T'NITE, I GOTTA! I GOTTA!

HERE'S WHAT I MAINLY WANNA SAY; FIRST THERE'S NO WAY G.E. SHOULD BE ALLOWED TO OWN NBC,* THEY GOT THIS HISTORY OF CORPORATE LAWBREAKING 'N' THERE'S TOO MUCH CHANCE THAT THEY MIGHT ALTER THE CONTENT A' THEIR NEWS SHOWS T' SUIT THEIR OWN PURPOSES. THERE'S A HEAVY CONFLICT A' INTEREST PROBLEM.

* LETTERMAN'S LATE NIGHT SHOW IS ON NBC, SO G.E. IS HIS BOSS.

LIKE G.E.'S A BIG DEFENSE CONTRACTOR. THEY GOT A BIG STAKE IN THIS STAR WARS PROGRAM, SO THEY MIGHT PROMOTE BIG DEFENSE SPENDING ON TV.

PLUS THEY'RE BEIN' SUED IN SOUTHERN OHIO FOR OVER ONE BILLION BUCKS FOR SELLING A DEFECTIVE NUCLEAR REACTOR THAT THEY KNEW FROM THEIR OWN INTERNAL REPORTS BACK IN 1975 OR EARLIER HAD A FLAWED DESIGN. EVEN THOUGH THEY KNEW ABOUT THE DESIGN PROBLEMS THEY WENT AHEAD AND SOLD IT ANYWAY, THEY SOLD A BUNCH OF 'EM ALL OVER THE COUNTRY WHICH'VE COST BILLIONS TO REPAIR. THINK THEY WANT TO PUBLICIZE THAT ON NBC NEWS?

THEN, THEIR MAN THAT THEY SENT OVER T'BE PRESIDENT A' NBC IN SEPTEMBER A' EIGHTY-SIX, ISSUES THIS SECRET MEMO IN NOVEMBER SAYIN' HE'S THINKING OF FORMING A POLITICAL ACTION COMMITTEE AT NBC AN' IMPLYIN' THAT HE'S GONNA BRING PRESSURE T'BEAR ON EMPLOYEES WHO DON'T JOIN IT... HEY, MAN, IT'S AGAINST FEDERAL ELECTION LAWS T'TRY T' COERCE PEOPLE T' JOIN A PAC.

AND HEY, MAN, I DON'T LIKE CONGLOMERATES IN GENERAL, BUT ESPECIALLY NOT G.E. THEY GOT A REALLY BAD HISTORY OF LAWBREAKING, AND THEY GOT WAY TOO MUCH POWER. THEY'RE A MILITARY-INDUSTRIAL-FINANCIAL-COMMUNICATIONS COMPLEX.

THE MILITARY-INDUSTRIAL COMPLEXES OF THE FIFTIES ARE TAME BY COMPARISON.

Chapter 4   **RECOVERING JEWISHNESS**

THE ACCEPTANCE OF COMICS AS A LEGITIMATE ART FORM HAS BEEN terribly long in coming, so long that twenty-first-century processes such as digital imaging would be unimaginable to even the most experimentally minded forebears. The delay gives comic art history an almost archaeological quality, as if crucial developments had taken place eons ago rather than mere generations ago. But one thing is fairly clear. If the breakthrough to formal acceptance bears one unmistakably Jewish name, that name surely is Art Spiegelman—for the contributions of *Raw* magazine to the redefinition of comics as art in the United States, first of all, but most especially for *Maus*, the two-volume literary sensation of collective and personal tragedy in Eastern Europe. In a way most curious even for the odd world of comic art at large, the totemic Jewish quality of a disobedient Holocaust saga with a slippery protagonist (the artist's father) became the unprecedented comic art-object. *Maus* had its own traveling exhibit, its own abundant scholarship, its own CD-ROM and Web site—in short, all the accoutrements of twenty-first-century popular art.[1]

The 2005–06 "Masters of American Comics" exhibit (and the accompanying lavish catalog) seemed to ignore the Jewish angle as far as possible, no easy task considering the personnel. That an emphatically Jewish-founded institution, the Hammer Museum of Los Angeles, was the original site of the exhibit (as it turns out, the only place it was displayed fully) and co-publisher of the volume makes the lack of emphasis even more obvious. One might argue that those acknowledged masters, Jack Kirby and Harvey Kurtzman, like so many lesser lights, for most of their careers simply chose assimilation. Jewish emphasis arrived at the logical juncture in Spiegelman's career and in Eisner's second beginning. Still, there was an odd sense of uncertain balance—what the literary scholars of the late twentieth century were inclined to call a "floating center"—to the whole enterprise.

Most uniquely, the "Masters" exhibit offered the public the artists' "roughs," from pencil drawings through various phases toward completion. This had not been done before, at least in any prominent way, for comics, although it has long since become standard for museum art and is increasingly a part of published art volumes. Comic artists had themselves only recognized the value of prepublication sketches when the drawings became collectibles on the Web, often after they had given the originals away, tossed them, or lost them. The notion that the preparatory material for the most vernacular of arts now had meaning (as well as commercial value) arrived slowly during the 1960s–90s, no doubt the result of the mainstream comic industry's creation of items specifically for collectors.

Not everyone, by any means, was happy with the "Masters" exhibit. Spiegelman pulled his own work from the final twin exhibition spaces of New York's Jewish Museum and the Newark Art Museum after assorted smaller conflicts along the way. This act by the exhibit's largest personal influence posed a question in many minds. If, according to an *Art News* critic, "comics are now officially an art form," then why *these* artists, exhibited in *this* fashion? The various issues—including an absence of women artists as well as a disproportionate number of Jewish artists—were not likely to go away.[2]

The resulting conversation about the "Masters" exhibit echoed in some ways the harsh words around the 1990 MoMA show "High and Low: Modern Art and Popular Culture." Comics were treated here as mere source material, the inspiration for "real artists" like Warhol and Lichtenstein, much as the scholarly use of oral history has treated interviews as raw data rather than expressions of orality with their own rules and logic. Spiegelman blasted the show as "dead high art . . . built on dead low art," with the vital, pulsing popular culture drained out and absent.[3] Thirteen years later, at a New York Historical Society panel accompanying a major retrospective on Jules Feiffer's career, some of the same issues arose, with Peter Kuper, Edward Sorel, Garry Trudeau, the *New Yorker*'s Roz Chast, and Frank Modell weighing in.

The panelists were, of course, happy to have comics and cartooning taken seriously under any rubric or rationalization. More often, this stamp of approval has happened through exhibits and forums on college campuses and events organized in greater New York by the (mostly virtual) Union Square headquarters of the Museum of Comic and Cartoon Art (which goes by the gourmet-coffee-sounding acronym MoCCA). Sometimes, and inevitably at Jewish institutions, the troubling question of Jewish identity within comics has continued to be posed. Mostly, as in the MoMA event of 1990, the "Jewish Question" seems to have eluded the Jewish presence, onstage and disproportionately among the audience.[4]

Whatever the causes and whatever the ongoing controversy, comics have now been raised up in the most respectable places as authentic art. The scholarship on seemingly esoteric points—such as the reintroduction of the dialogue bubble in the comics of the 1890s after it had been abandoned for two generations, compelling the audience to read dialogue in addition to observing the *action* of the characters—has now been steadily elaborated. We understand better that the pursuit of and ongoing rapport with the mass audience created the comic form as we know it, even as the newspapers fade and the comic artists pursue Art.[5]

How much does it matter? Newfound respectability may not have aided the average comic artist or scriptwriter all that much, apart from a psychological boost. The ordinary life of the comic craftsperson revealed itself once more, in 2007, when a prestigious Harvey Pekar quipped laconically that his own archived stick-figure-in-panel scripts might indeed be worth real money someday—"but only after I'm dead!"[6]

This was pretty much the reality for *most* of the artists outside the golden circles of newspaper syndication and comic book management, going back several generations: they didn't live long enough to be pronounced "artists," and they never got paid all that much. They were, by a considerable majority, Jewish tradesmen who labored in personal obscurity (however popular some of their characters were), not unlike the skilled Jewish tradesmen from so many generations and centuries before them who were recognized in their art, if not their names, by modernists Marc Chagall and El Lissitzky, who surveyed ancient Russian synagogues during the late 1910s.[7] The comic book artisans were who they were, doing the best art allowed, the best art possible under the circumstances. Their Jewish identity was a private thing because alternatives did not exist. Things have now changed, at least to a considerable degree; some Jewish artists take advantage of the changes, while others have chosen the familiar assimilation path for their own reasons.

Once more, how much does it matter? Well, at least it matters to those of us who are interested in comic art and comics as art, and doubtless to the dignity of the practitioners. Perhaps that is enough after all.

THERE IS GOOD REASON not to separate the critical upgrade, whatever its personal effects, from larger trends of Jewishness within popular culture. Just over a half-century ago, in 1956, a MoMA show on animation, the first in any art museum, had featured the work of UPA, a group of Hollywood liberal left-wingers in a field heavily Jewish, on the verge of being blacklisted but self-described in no way as Jewish. To do so, as in Hollywood, would only underline the risk. With the easing of restrictions, things began to change. The uncloseting of Jewish identity in television and film from the 1960s onward had an impact that was commercially proven and therefore artistically possible. Only close observers (or anti-Semites) thought very much about Roseanne Barr being Jewish, if they knew she was at all, and her rage at Judaism as a patriarchal religion during 2007 came as a painful surprise but hardly an unprecedented one. Jerry Seinfeld and *The Simpsons'* Krusty the Clown, as well as Larry David, Jon Stewart, and others among Barr's colleagues in nightly syndication, were something else, by-products of an accelerating process tending beyond what some Jewish intellectuals have called "normalization," the acceptance of Jews as Jews with no special (negative) qualities.

Historically speaking, the normalization trend should have been easiest to spot within the revival of the mainstream comic book field, except for the notable factor of continued Jewish invisibility. Comics writer, editor, and historian Danny Fingeroth, in his book *Disguised as Clark Kent: Jews, Comics, and the Creation of the Superhero*, argues that the new Justice Society of America, along with the entire Julius Schwartz–edited DC line, was pervaded by subtle Jewish themes of the Holocaust and the more hopeful future. No character bore a Jewish name, and most readers could be forgiven for missing the subtleties. Big sales at DC led to a grander vision at Marvel, largely Stan Lee's own brainchild by that time. Lee and Jack Kirby invented the Fantastic Four, who were notable for existing in New York City (rather than Gotham or Metropolis), for being regularly involved with story lines that deal with memory/identity problems, and above all for wearing their neuroses on their super-sleeves.[8] Spider-Man, arguably, embodied all those themes of urban, ethnic alienation; meanwhile the Hulk was referred to as the "Green Golem" and Captain America turned out to have been a World War II "survivor" whose early friends were dead.[9]

Fingeroth makes another central point likely lost on younger readers: Marvel superheroes lived in a lower-middle-class, Jewish Manhattan, not yet suburbanized but a long way from the urban poverty of the 1910s–30s. How did this relate to the status of the Jewish artists? Unlike the owners of the companies (and of the lucrative properties that had been created as works-for-hire), most were able to find some measure of prosperity only through leaving the business, or through taking on backbreaking quantities of work—if they could still get it. Some removed themselves, like a large chunk of the Jewish population, to L.A., finding their skills well suited to the animation industry, which, however, turned out not to pay a whole lot better than comics. Many old-timers on both coasts found themselves doing the convention circuit, selling sketches and reproductions of their early work to fans eager to meet and purchase mementoes of the men (and a few women) whose work they had grown up on. Many moved into advertising, which by the 1950s was opening up seriously to Jewish artists and writers. Still others, like Joe Simon, co-creator (with Jack Kirby) of Captain America in the 1940s, moved laterally in the publishing world, essentially creating the romance genre and the slightly edgy *Mad* imitation *Sick*.[10]

The more adventurous of the younger artists and writers of the 1970s leaned as far in the direction of the avant-garde as the format and the boss would permit. The return of noir in American cinema prompted new characters and new styles. A hard-core Jewish "adventure" character, Dominic

Fortune (né David Fortunov), was more sexual than previous generations had been allowed, his wisecracks less likely to be throwaway lines. His creator was Howard Chaykin, best known for the early 1980s invention of the sci-fi comic *American Flagg!* Chaykin let interviewers know, from time to time, that he harbored deep anticorporate sentiments. Fingeroth, who did some writing on Fortune/Fortunov, notes that the character was rejected for secret government projects because of his compulsive gambling, his love life, and his Jewishness.[11]

Elsewhere in the comics mainstream, that perpetual rarity, an explicitly Jewish character—Flatbush's own Izzy Cohen—actually appeared in the mid-1960s within the absurdly militaristic *Sgt. Fury and His Howling Commandos*.[12] A few years later, Gentile artist Jim Steranko invented Sidney A. Levine, "the brains"—that is, a mechanical genius—for the *S.H.I.E.L.D.* series. And so on. During the decades to follow, careful readers could cite more than forty outright Jewish characters, including Holocaust survivors, an occasional Jewish lesbian, and even an Israeli ambassador! Most curiously, however, amid all this, typically Jewish names remained relatively rare within mainstream comics, as if the next generations did not want to stray too far and alienate readers.[13]

Meanwhile, the comic print trade suffered. Superheroes, with the largest presence in popular culture by the 1990s that they had held since World War II, were overwhelmingly consumed by audiences everywhere *but* in comic books, which had become a niche hobbyists' medium. Movies and television, but increasingly video games and licensed kids' product lines (lunch boxes, Halloween costumes, and so on) had taken over the comic franchises.[14]

But on the edges of the mainstream, things began to change dramatically and, from the looks of things, irreversibly in any number of related ways. If Milton Caniff's bemuscled Aryan-looking world conquerors had arguably been the *least* Jewish of characters during the Cold War years, *Zippy the Pinhead* involved some of the most Jewish of settings and references (drawn by Gentile Bill Griffith, largely based on his Long Island childhood) of the last decades of the twentieth century and beyond. Zippy, not syndicated widely, was only the small tip of a wedge that got into the mainstream.[15] Further into the margin, in the syndicated strips of the alternative press from the early 1990s, was unarguably the most Yiddishist strip since the Yiddish strips themselves and, along with Spiegelman's work, arguably the most self-consciously Jewish work on the printed page. It was *Cheap Novelties*, and the artist was Ben Katchor.

Here we enter a special world, interestingly by way of both the old Left and the avant-garde. Katchor, born in 1960, grew up with a Yiddish-speaking father so elderly that he'd lost a previous family in the Holocaust, and so bound to left-wing tradition that he served on the fund-raising board of the Yiddish newspaper *Morgn Frayhayt*. It happened to be the fading tabloid of former communists who insisted upon the highest of Yiddish literary standards—with the fewest concessions to Americanisms—anywhere in the American Jewish world.

Katchor is the comic strip artist sui generis, or perhaps in another way marks the emergence of the art school graduate (or nongraduate) who renders a fresh painting in each panel. By marked contrast to familiar cartoonish styles, his figuration in gray wash recalls the return of representational styles during the early 1960s after the hegemony of abstract expressionism. His work looks a bit like Ben Shahn with a dash of Larry Rivers. Katchor has said that his dialogue owes much to forerunners like Harry Hershfield, but no one else was likely to interpret Hershfield in this way, with sideways glances in place of knee-slapping gags. His appearance to a wider comic readership in *Raw* was a perfect fit.

Looking at Katchor's world and then back at the underground comix art that served as a vivid and vernacular counterpart to canvas for the 1960s–70s generation suggests a host of other subtle connections. Somewhere behind the transgressive sex and dope themes could be found some of the best artists' referencing of a fragmented and disappearing urbanism.

The genetically Gentile but Judeophilic R. Crumb's artistic rambles begin in Cleveland in the early 1960s, with the past etched in tenement skylines and oddball characters alongside the anonymous art of outdated storefront signs and advertising logos. He was hanging out with Harvey Pekar and, shortly, married a local Jewish girl. Likewise, arguably, Bill Griffith's work is rooted in 1950s–60s Long Island, where he was raised within the garishness created by suburban devastation. Not born with Jewishness, he was assimilated into it. For half-Jewish Justin Green, it's the Near North Side of Chicago in more or less the same era that taught him the accents and angles. Pekar, of course, has gone on capturing in the urban memories of a wounded Cleveland the vanished generation of legendarily short and furiously gregarious lower-middle-class Jewish guys, in particular those who spoke for hours with self-created authority on any given topic, from politics to baseball.

Katchor recalls the particulars of that all-but-vanished world better than anyone else, freely inventing as he goes along. *Cheap Novelties: The Pleasures of Urban Decay* (1991) introduced his fairly long-lasting protagonist Julius (whose surname is the Yiddish word *"knipl,"* the pocket money needed by a working-class or lower-middle-class Jew of earlier generations to get through the day, or a little adventure), a real estate photographer who so observes the passing scene as to make himself part of it. *Julius Knipl, Real Estate Photographer: Stories* (1996) and *The Beauty Supply District* (2000) completed a vision that nevertheless remains to be elaborated on endlessly. Sometimes it takes place in the vacation spots Jewish New Yorkers were said to love most, the Catskills in one direction or a pseudoretro quasi–Miami Beach (he places something very much like South Beach upon an unknown island, perhaps off the Florida coast) in the other.

It is not so much the predictable characters but a spirit of anonymous invention that delight—details of popular culture always fresh and always familiar. Katchor is not so much satirizing as offering an enigmatic commentary on displacement. Yiddish editor, culture critic, and pedagogue Itche Goldberg—before his 2006 death known as the eldest author anywhere to bring out a new book (literary criticism, at age 101)—famously interpreted the paradoxical Jewish nostalgia for roots in the era of the rebellious break from older traditions as "remembering remembering."

Seeing Katchor in these terms contrasts with the self-conscious avant-gardism of Spiegelman, by the 1990s the senior underground cartoonist of note (along with Crumb, Griffith, and a few others), and by then also a *New Yorker* illustrator of both political controversy and artistic acclaim. As for many other Holocaust survivors' children, the darkness of the soul is Spiegelman's best element, although the artist's sheer inventiveness with form and color would suggest to some readers, including a sometimes grumpy Harvey Pekar, that *Maus* constituted a retreat to what could sell.[16]

That would be, of course, a misunderstanding. Back in the days of the underground comix, when Spiegelman was only emerging from LSD visions to a commentary on his mother's suicide's effect upon him, col-

lective memory took on fresh comic forms in his art. As literary scholar
Deborah Geis observes, the "problem of representation" of the Holocaust
for those who did not experience it has been a major trope in Jewish art of
all kinds; Theodore Adorno had warned against it, early on, as a violation
("There can be no poetry after Auschwitz"), but one in which Jewish artists
across the world found themselves participating unavoidably and as a matter of course.[17]

No one, at any rate, had ever done it Spiegelman's way or even imagined it possible. In part, *Maus* was oral history, son Art writing down
father-survivor Vladek's stories in Rego Park, Brooklyn, during the 1960s–
70s, rendering the people as "funny animals," Jews as mice, Germans as
cats, and (occasionally) Poles as pigs. Spiegelman had all kinds of emotional problems with his father, who was none too pleasant to his second
wife, Mala; demanded physical assistance in ways that the artist could
hardly provide; and viewed commercial success as the only reason to work.
Vladek was one of the interwar Jewish wheeler-dealers who survived when
the more humane and vulnerable perished, and bore not a trace of survivor's guilt or moral lesson. He had a low view of black people, which is
to say that the transference of oppression and suffering meant nothing to
him. Not that Vladek was so unusual. But Spiegelman utterly defied the
canonization of the survivors nurtured in what has come to be called Holocaust kitsch.

An extraordinary work, indeed the work of a lifetime, *Maus* is destined
to go on being extraordinary for no one more than for the artist himself.
Spiegelman's only completed full-length work (apart from children's books
and illustrating writers' texts) all these years later, it carries the magnitude
of the effort and the weight of the accomplishment. Otherwise, Spiegelman is at his strongest with political jabs at the establishment, especially
the authoritarian Rudolph Giuliani regime close to home, making Spiegelman, for a moment or two, the most controversial comic strip artist in
Manhattan in recent generations. Later, he extended his polemic against
George W. Bush and the Bushies in and around the White House, coura-
geously making common cause with the political militants of *World War 3
Illustrated*.

Arguably and understandably, nothing but the memory of the Holocaust fixed the artist's attention so firmly until the towers of 9/11, for which

Spiegelman felt compelled to re-create his artistic methods, ultimately returning to a handful of images from early twentieth-century comic strips like *Maggie and Jiggs*, now imaginatively reworked in the light of modern horror. Never having precisely one fixed method in the way that other comic artists almost invariably develop, Spiegelman was free to try, then fail, to satisfy himself, and then try again until he found what satisfied him. Most of the resulting volume was made up of what had been called color plates, the originals from the Sunday golden age of newspaper comic strips.

In the Shadow of No Towers was, then, a sinking of self into comics lore, both escape and visual bible. Here, in an increasingly troubled world, he found respite and meaning. It was also his way of saying good-bye to the *New Yorker*, to Spiegelman's eye a growingly complacent magazine but also his major outlet for a decade and his entrée into high-culture America. He was on his own again in that sense at least, experimenting widely, producing children's books, anthologies, and a run of his own other assorted work.[18]

But so much had changed in only a decade. By the mid-1990s and perhaps before, Spiegelman and Griffith had seemingly eclipsed Crumb, the artistic exile living in the south of France whose enduring fame, especially among younger generations, might be attributed to the 1994 documentary film directed by Crumb's old friend Terry Zwigoff.[19] The filmmaker seemingly neglected the emergence of an inner, intensely Jewish logic in Crumb's *Introducing Kafka* (1994), toward whose preparation Crumb and his literary collaborator David Zane Mairowitz had turned their attention during the years Zwigoff documented.

Nevertheless, *Introducing Kafka* was a masterpiece of illustration and was, at least to many readers, Crumb's best work since the 1970s, as well as his most creative: like one or two of the Yiddish comic artists, he had moved over into illustration of the text, and here he found another self. *"Introduction to . . ."* books had been appearing for twenty years, but the genre had faded. None, it is safe to say, had more psychological depth than *Kafka*, and the Crumb/Mairowitz team captured a Jewishness that many Kafka critics somehow avoided or persisted in seeing in terms of religion, Zionism, and all sorts of matters rather than the vanished world of the European diasporic Jew.

Not only did Crumb brilliantly draw Kafka as a doomed European Jew, an artist with a dark and penetrating view, but he also made an unrelenting critique of the post-Holocaust, post-Stalinist capitalistic society determined to celebrate itself and its rampant materialism. In Mairowitz's words, the tragedy of Kafka's Czechoslovakia under the Austrians, Germans, and Russians has been succeeded by the "fake American dream." A Prague of giant advertising billboards, SUVs, carbon monoxide clouds, Kafka T-shirts, and Kafkaburgers is closer to Kafka's real vision than anyone but the author and artist wanted to admit seeing.

Crumb's unwonted (and perhaps unwanted) appearance on the cover of *Art News* in September 2004 marked the elevation of his work on the art market, whose evaluation of his work he had sought to avoid all these decades. Now a restaurant-napkin doodle of his drawings apparently sold for $35,000 as the artist continued to avoid anything approaching celebrity. The positive side of all this was the series of Crumb retrospectives in prestigious art galleries across the United States and in Europe. (The priciest was, naturally, in Pittsburgh's Carnegie Gallery, founded on the largesse of just the sort of robber baron whom Crumb had been cursing since the 1960s.) So he, too, continued down his own path, this time toward an adaptation of the biblical Book of Genesis.

Among those Jewish alternative artists producing and selling continuously, we next find Larry Gonick, math graduate of Harvard in the 1960s, short-time underground comix artist, and longtime creator of "cartoon histories" (actually, comic histories) of everything from world history to galactic history, with lots in between. In the cartoon histories, Gonick found himself particularly at home as a Jew illustrating Old Testament stories. His stories were funny, with their serious debunking of historical myths, but also explanatory in key ways. Gonick later turned more toward the popularization of science, but in his two-score volumes and counting he has never ceased exercising his wit to satirize the system, he has never greatly altered his brilliantly explanatory style, and he has never stopped producing.[20]

After these giants with roots in the 1960s comes Peter Kuper, a generation younger. The Kuper story might logically begin with *Mad* magazine, because Kuper has taken over the "Spy vs. Spy" page in recent years and is widely considered the magazine's star contributor. Or it could start with Harvey Pekar, because Cleveland homeboy Kuper met R. Crumb through Pekar and found encouragement from him to launch his comics career with a fanzine.

Kuper was, from the time he picked up a pen, on the leftward edge of social observation. He made his living in New York as a flunky at *Richie Rich* (later reframing the images for "Richie Bush," one of the most scathing of his antiwar, anti-Bush satires), but his avocation was the political zine *World War 3 Illustrated*, founded with fellow Clevelander Seth Tobocman in 1980 and managing something over an issue per year ever since with a host of contributors and an ever-shifting, substantially Jewish editorial group. Nibbling at the edges of mainstream status for decades, Kuper has also been one of the most inventive of artists, adopting one style after another to suit the current tasks and his own interest.

Kuper did his version of Kafka, an adaptation of *The Metamorphosis* with no Crumb-like figure about and no sex (or even full-blooded women), just the horror in the soul of the author. But he has done some of his most fascinating work in color, notably a full-color adaptation of Upton Sinclair's *The Jungle* and a series of remarkable children's books (the most recent, *Theo and the Blue Note*, explains jazz through color patterns more than story line). The semi-autobiographical *Stop Forgetting to Remember* (2007) also qualifies, a semi-colored, sepia leaking into scatterings of pages, then disappearing again, defining time shifts, moods, and fantasies.[21]

Kuper's political comrade Seth Tobocman might be described as a street fighter of an artist. A longtime political squatter-activist on the Lower East Side in the anti-gentrification early 1990s, as well as a militant antiglobalization and antiwar activist, Tobocman puts the rage in the page (thus his aptly titled 1999 collection *You Don't Have to Fuck People Over to Survive*), but he also has reflective moments, as in *Portraits of Israelis and Palestinians* (2003), with sketches Kuper made during a visit to the Middle East, to present, as he explains to his parents, the humanity of all sides. *Disaster and Resistance* (2008), his latest collection, continues this work with a remarkable glimpse of New Orleans post-Katrina, seen close at hand.[22] He is, in short, altogether the kind of artist that German revolutionaries of the 1920s could have called their own. Humor has not been his strong suit, but personal commitment to humanism, absolute and unlimited, most definitely has.[23]

A third early activist with *World War 3 Illustrated*, Eric Drooker, artist of *Street Posters and Ballads* (1995) "with an afterword by Allen Ginsberg," carried the militant message and took it in a different direction.[24] Ginsberg himself was drawn to Drooker first by the artist's posters in Tompkins Square Park and then by Drooker's loving illuminations of Ginsberg's works. Drooker proved an eco-visionary of transhistorical human experience with *Flood! A Novel in Pictures* (1992), one of the most remarkable works of the new generation. A native Manhattanite, born in 1958 and removed to Berkeley in the new century, Drooker is a yet more severe expressionist responding suitably to the extreme conditions of life and love on the planet.

Bob Fingerman, product of Rego Park (where Spiegelman's father lived and died) and of the School of Visual Arts in the last years when Harvey Kurtzman was still teaching, became one of those few lucky enough to collaborate with the master. Fingerman went on to work for the enduring *Mad* knockoff *Cracked*, then *Penthouse Hot Talk* (that is, soft porn), leading eventually to a widely praised graphic novel, *Beg the Question* (1999), a reworked collection drawn from his comic book series *Minimum Wage*. *Beg the Question* was definitely the life of the alternative comic artist working on the edges of porn magazines (whose exploitative entrepreneurs include a true-to-life Al Goldstein) to hack out a living, but mainly about various personal relationships, from friendship and roommate-hood to love and marriage.

Cut to James Sturm, part of the generation for whom comic art transcends politics and personal experience. His own mini-academy, the Center for Cartoon Studies, in the modest Yankee village of White River Junction, Vermont, is now turning out the newest comic prospects. Sturm sees himself as less politically engaged than, say, the artists of *World War 3 Illustrated*, and this sets him apart from the underground generation as well. What interests Sturm foremost is the art form and using it to tell very specific stories in which historical fiction and nonfiction merge.[25]

"The Golem's Mighty Swing," a comic novelette making up sixty tinted pages of a volume within a larger volume, *James Sturm's America: God, Gold, and Golems* (2007), is doubtless Sturm's magnum opus thus far. In one sense it is pure 1920s Americana, set in the era of the traveling baseball teams playing locals for personal glory and a little cash. Few of the players will ever make the majors, most certainly not the superb nonwhite athletes. Our protagonists, the bearded Stars of David, offer one example of these low-cost operations. They are up-front Jews in a nation where anti-Semitism is open and aggressive, where the KKK holds power in at least a half-dozen states, and where not even a Catholic could be elected president. The Stars have only one real star: a huge, veteran black hitter passing as Jewish. At the urging of an enterprising PR man, he becomes "The Golem."

What's most interesting here is not the story, which is well told and even realistic, but the art itself. One could call it "flat," but that would mistake affect for intention. Sturm, unlike Seth Tobocman, mostly avoids melodrama, even amid violence. In this and several other respects, Sturm is rather like Jason Lutes, a native New Jerseyan born in 1967 and educated at the Rhode Island School of Design, but also for a time an art director of an alternative weekly in Seattle. Lutes's signal triumph has been the many-part series *Berlin*, a look at the Central European center of sophisticated culture shortly before Hitler took power. Full of personal details with relatively little dialogue and more still figures than action, it might rightly be seen as a black-and-white painting on the printed page. With the first eight issues finally anthologized in 2001 and two more anthologies planned, *Berlin* is a triumphant successor to Lutes's serialized feature *Jar of Fools: A Picture Story*, which gained more visibility in its 2003 reprint. The saga of a magician down on his luck, it might have seemed a Depression-era drama except for the appearance of a television set and superhighways.[26] Social relations are bad, an aging mentor is the only character who arguably looks Jewish, and owing, perhaps, to the serialized format of the original, mysteries are never solved. In *Houdini: The Handcuff King* (2007), the Jewish escape artist does not finally escape himself or his own special fate.[27]

Without a shred of didacticism, Lutes and Sturm are political despite themselves, by the power of the imagination and the pen. To say that they have triumphed over either the didacticism or the displaced Jewishness of Kuper, Tobocman, Drooker, or Schulman would be mistaken. They are perhaps *di yunge* to the Yiddish socialists, almost a century later. But the original *di yunge* writers, young proletarian poets, also had a politics, including a politics of form. There is no right or wrong here as Jewish artists, among others, face the crises of the new century. Each shall find his or her own way.

Some of the brightest new lights would go still further with an aesthetic, they insist, wholly divorced from any particular social content. The most influential under-thirty figure—though his influence is felt more in his work as an editor than as an artist—is Sammy Harkham, born to Jewish immigrants in Los Angeles who moved the family to Australia when he was fourteen. There he fell in love with comics, before his return to L.A. Since the early years of the new century he has been publishing issues of *Kramer's Ergot*, viewed by some close observers, notably Art Spiegelman, as the most remarkable comics anthology to appear since *Raw*. A recent *Kramer's Ergot* offers up the editor's own version of nineteenth-century shtetl life among the Lubavitchers. Only *Mendy and the Golem*, a short-lived comic published in the spirit of Hasidism, has gone further in expressed piety.[28]

But the other sort of Jewish and Jewish American traditions are never far behind. Perhaps it was inevitable that a collection of comics on teenage life would bring precocious Jewish girls out of the artistic woodwork to recall the anxieties that they consider their own. Two young artists, Vanessa Davis and Lauren Weinstein, have turned out streams of memories and commentaries about family, friends, crushes on boys, sexy fantasies, bitter disappointments, and middle-class life's assorted problems.[29] In marked contrast, Miriam Libicki, born in 1981 in white-bread Columbus, Ohio, left the United States for Israel in the early years of the new century, then moved to Vancouver and created a comic series of her own, *Jobnik!*, about her experiences working for the Israel Defense Force (IDF), along with a peacenik project, *Ceasefire*. Her memory of the gender contradictions within the IDF may be her most unique contribution thus far; she approaches her work with no particular political slant, just as she experienced her life as a young woman in a short-term aliyah.

Other comic artists grapple with elements of Jewish history, looking for ways to explain connections absent from the usual literary and corporate success stories. Gangsterism is definitely back, no doubt on the heels of films and popular histories involving Jewish *shtarkers*, or tough guys, long an embarrassment in literature, now more likely to be a point of pride. Joe Kubert, doyen of the superhero mainstream long past and founder of a little school carrying his own name, reemerged in a different light with *Yossel*, a sketchbook about the Warsaw Ghetto Uprising of 1943, and *Jew Gangster*, a rock 'em, sock 'em tale of a very un-Jewish-looking youngster and his rise in the Mob during the 1930s. *Jew Gangster* pales by comparison, in both art and narration, to the remarkable *Brownsville: A Graphic*

Novel, by comic writer (and artist) Neil Kleid and artist Jake Allen (who took classes at Kubert's school), and the generational difference seems crucial. If Kubert closes with the crypto-message that Jews in modern times must have guns, Kleid and Allen close, like Will Eisner does in his late work, in the multicultural New York that succeeds the world of the ghettoized Jews of the past.[30]

Enter, finally, Miriam Katin, a Holocaust survivor, for a time an Israeli animation worker, then a children's book illustrator in New York and a commercial artist. In 2006, she published her first graphic novel, *We Are on Our Own*. It is her own family story, reconstructed from a collective memory (because so little family documentation remains) and rendered in an etching style little seen in comics but as suitable in its dark-toned realism as Spiegelman's imaginative, unfunny animal workings. The story is literally of how the world deserted them, these Jews abandoned or, worse, fingered by their Gentile neighbors and fellow city-dwellers. They must flee, leaving every trace of memory behind, disguising themselves as the Gentiles who hate them. If no art is equal to this subject, Katin's has a remarkable depth of intent and execution. It may well be the final word of a Holocaust survivor in fully-realized comic form.[31]

FROM AARGH! TO ZAP! Harvey Kurtzman's *Visual History of the Comics* (1991) must have been, like all of Kurtzman's works, an intended money-maker, a book with many pictures and not too many words, given a master's touch by the founder of *Mad* and the inspiration for so much more. But it seems to have evolved toward a summing of a lifetime's experience in comic art. Kurtzman grew too ill, however, to complete the work, finished at last by a distinguished nonacademic scholar of animation. The last chapter, "Comics as Art," offered what seems to be Kurtzman's tribute to his successors, and in particular to Art Spiegelman, his literal successor at the School of Visual Arts (still later instructors would include Peter Kuper, Ben Katchor, and Kim Deitch). Kurtzman closed a thought with the phrase "grown-ups can read 'Maus' and feel a respect for Spiegelman's writing; they can read 'Maus' as if they were reading a novel."[32] He had, perhaps, been waiting a lifetime for this kind of appreciation of his own generation's work, and time had run out before the rich stages of development ahead in the new century. But the time had indeed come, at last, with Jewishness of many kinds embedded in the subject, suitable for exploration for a long time to come. The master of the field in so many ways died with that consolation, at least.

"Strip Mauled Again" by Bill Griffith, from *Zippy Annual
2002* (Seattle: Fantagraphics Books, 2002). Reprinted by
permission of the artist.

The Cartoon History of the Universe by Larry Gonick (San Francisco: RipOff Press, 1979). Reprinted by permission of the artist.

WE MAY WELL DOUBT THE STORY OF MOSES' BIRTH ✿, BUT THIS MUCH SEEMS CERTAIN: "MOSES" IS AN EGYPTIAN NAME; MOSES WAS RAISED IN COURT AS AN EGYPTIAN; AND HE MUST HAVE HAD FORMAL, "COOL" EGYPTIAN MANNERS. LET'S IMAGINE HIM, THEN, AS *HALF EGYPTIAN,* A BIT OF A LONER, WITH A LOT OF RE-PRESSED ANGER, WHICH HE COULDN'T ALWAYS CONTROL.

IN THE FIRST REPORTED EPISODE OF HIS ADULT LIFE, MOSES THREW A TANTRUM AND *MURDERED* AN OVER-SEER FOR ABUSING THE SLAVES.

JACKAL! WITLESS HIPPO! TAKE THAT AND THAT AND THAT!

CRAK BASH SMUSH

?

HE SKIPPED THE COUNTRY AND TOOK REFUGE WITH *JETHRO,* A MIDIANITE CHIEF IN THE SINAI.

AN EGYPTIAN PRINCE!

UH, ACTUALLY, I'M HALF HEBREW...

BLESS ME! SO AM I!

JETHRO MUST HAVE FILLED THE FUGITIVE IN ON LOCAL HISTORY, POLITICS, AND RELIGION — INCLUDING HIS OWN ROOTS!

IT IS SAID — HE WHO WIELDS THIS *BRAZEN SERPENT* WILL FREE THE PEOPLE OF ABRAHAM!

JETHRO ALSO GAVE MOSES HIS DAUGHTER *ZIPPORAH.*

WOW! A REAL *EGYPTIAN PRINCE!*

TH' SHAME OF IT! ME AND THIS NOMAD SHE-CAMEL!... SIGH...

✿ WE'VE ALL HEARD HOW THE BABY MOSES WAS CAST ADRIFT ON THE NILE, BUT BEFORE BELIEVING IT, WE SHOULD CONSIDER THAT THE ABANDONED-BABY-WHO-BECOMES-KING THEME ALSO APPEARS IN THE LIVES OF SARGON OF AKKAD, OEDIPUS REX, CYRUS OF PERSIA, ROMULUS+REMUS, AND OTHERS. MANY SCHOLARS BELIEVE THE STORY WAS INVENTED BY "OFFICIAL BIOGRAPHERS" TO GIVE THESE PRINCES THE RIGHT PARENTS.

THUS, IF MOSES WERE ACTUALLY AN *EGYPTIAN,* THE BULRUSHES STORY SERVES TO MAKE HIM ⸘PUF PUF⸘ AN *HONORARY HEBREW!*

BUT REALLY IT'S JUST SO MUCH *BULRUSH,* MIGHT ONE SAY?

NOT IF ONE WANTS TENURE AT YALE...

ON THE OTHER HAND, IT'S TRUE THAT PEOPLE OFTEN EXPOSED UNWANTED BABIES IN THOSE DAYS, SO WHO KNOWS?

'BYE, SON! HAVE A NICE TIME IN THE *PALACE!!*

YOU WON'T FORGET WHO GAVE YOU YOUR FIRST BIG *BREAK?*

"Mike Bloomfield" by Justin Green, from *Musical Legends* (San Francisco: Last Gasp, 2006). Reprinted by permission of the artist.

137

From "God in a Cave" by Peter Kuper, reprinted from *Blab!* 11 (Seattle: Fantagraphics Books, 2003) by permission of the artist.

"David and Goliath" by Eric Drooker, reprinted from *World War 3 Illustrated #10: Fascism* (1988) by permission of the artist.

THE KING WAS WELL FED AND GREW BIGGER EVERY DAY

ONE DAY A SMALL BOY SLUNG A STONE AT THE KING

WHO SHOT THE LITTLE BOY THROUGH THE HEART

AND THE KING ORDERED HIS SOLDIERS TO BREAK ALL THE LITTLE BOYS' HANDS

SO THEY COULD NEVER THROW STONES AT HIM EVER EVER AGAIN

"The Serpent of State" by Seth Tobocman, from *Disasters and Resistance: Political Comics* (Oakland: AK Press, 2008). Reprinted by permission of the artist.

BUT WAIT, THERE IS NEW CONSTRUCTION GOING ON IN THIS VILLAGE. AT FIRST IT APPEARS THE ISRAELIS ARE BUILDING....

...A LONG HIGHWAY WITH A DEEP DITCH NEXT TO IT.

IF BARBED WIRE IS ADDED, THE ROAD BECOMES A FENCE.

THEN, IN PLACES, CEMENT AND GUARD TOWERS ARE ADDED. THE ISRAELIS ARE BUILDING A WALL IN PALESTINE.

THEY SAY THIS WALL IS FOR THE SECURITY OF ISRAEL.

BUT THE WALL DOES NOT FOLLOW THE GREEN LINE, THE INTER-NATIONALLY RECOGNIZ-ED BORDER OF ISRAEL

INSTEAD, IT SNAKES AROUND THE LARGER SETTLE-MENTS.

THE WALL WILL SEPARATE PALESTINIAN FARMERS FROM THEIR LAND

IN OTHER PLACES THE WALL WILL LOCK PALESTINIANS INTO A NO-MAN'S LAND WHERE THEY WILL BE NIETHER ISRAELI NOR PALESTINIAN CITIZENS AND SO HAVE NO LEGAL RIGHTS.

JEWBLACKJEWBLACKJEWBLACKJEWBLACKJEWBLACK!

LOOKING BACK AT THE CHAOS AND CONFUSION OF THE PAST YEAR, WITH ITS SPIRAL OF FEAR & CONTEMPT, I FEEL A GROWING SENSE OF UNEASE....

TENSION BETWEEN BLACKS & JEWS HAS REACHED AN ALL-TIME HIGH...WHILE I CAN SYMPATHIZE WITH THE RESENTMENT BLACKS MUST FEEL, I ALSO RELATE TO THE OUTRAGE JEWS FEEL—BEING ONE MYSELF.

FOR YEARS BLACKS HAVE BEEN ANGRY AT THE PREFERENTIAL TREATMENT JEWS RECEIVED IN HOUSING & OTHER CITY SERVICES, WHILE JEWS BLAME BLACKS FOR A RISE IN NEIGHBORHOOD CRIME, VIOLENCE & ANTI-SEMITISM.

THIS ANGER HAS REACHED A BOILING POINT IN CROWN HEIGHTS, BROOKLYN...

THE PERCEPTION THAT JEWISH PEOPLE ENJOY PRIVILEGES DENIED AFRICAN AMERICANS IS ACCURATE. BECAUSE MOST JEWS ARE CONSIDERED "WHITE"—AND AMERICA IS A RACIST SOCIETY—JEWS EXPERIENCE AN ECONOMIC MOBILITY THAT SHUTS OUT BLACKS....

FIFTY YEARS AGO, HOWEVER, THROUGHOUT EUROPE JEWS WERE NOT CONSIDERED WHITE, BUT A "MONGREL RACE" WHO THREATENED WHITE SUPREMACY....

THEY WERE ROUNDED UP AND MADE INTO SLAVES WHOSE LABOR WOULD HELP BUILD HITLER'S "NEW ORDER." MILLIONS WERE WORKED TO DEATH...

MILLIONS OF AFRICANS WERE WORKED TO DEATH IN THIS COUNTRY...THIS "AMERICAN HOLOCAUST" CONTINUES TO PLAGUE BLACK AMERICANS IN THE FORM OF POVERTY, UNEMPLOYMENT, HOMELESSNESS, POLICE BRUTALITY, ETC....

JEWISH PEOPLE HAVE "MADE IT" IN AMERICA. FOR THE TIME BEING THEY ARE TREATED AS HONORARY WHITES—BUT THIS CAN ALWAYS CHANGE... MEANWHILE THEY FIND THEMSELVES PITTED AGAINST AFRICAN AMERICANS WHO ARE TOTALLY FED UP WITH THE DOUBLE STANDARD OF JUSTICE.

I WONDER WHAT THE FUTURE HOLDS...WILL WE SEE EACH OTHER AS POTENTIAL ALLIES—OR BE BLINDED BY RAGE?

© MCMXCII DROOKER

"JEWBLACK" by Eric Drooker, reprinted from *World War 3 Illustrated* #18. By permission of the artist.

"Heartburn and Heart Attack" scripted by David Greenberger and drawn by J.R. Williams, from *No More Shaves: a Duplex Planet Collection* (Seattle: Fantagraphic Books, 2003), with permission of writer and artist.

"Rabbi Story" by Bob Fingerman, from *Beg the Question* (Seattle: Fantagraphic Books, 2005). Reprinted by permission of the artist.

From *MAUS, a Survivor's Tale, I* by Art Spiegelman (New York: Pantheon, 1986). Reprinted by permission of the artist.

147

EVERYONE CAME VERY NICE DRESSED. THEY TRIED SO THAT THEY WOULD LOOK YOUNG AND ABLE TO WORK, IN ORDER TO GET A GOOD STAMP ON THEIR PASSPORT.

WHEN WE WERE EVERYBODY INSIDE, GESTAPO WITH MACHINE GUNS SURROUNDED THE STADIUM.

LINE UP BY FAMILY AT THE TABLES TO REGISTER! QUICKLY!

THEN WAS A SELECTION, WITH PEOPLE SENT EITHER TO THE LEFT, EITHER TO THE RIGHT.

OLD PEOPLE, FAMILIES WITH LOTS OF KIDS, AND PEOPLE WITHOUT WORK CARDS ARE ALL GOING TO THE LEFT!

WE UNDERSTOOD THIS MUST BE VERY BAD.

ME AND ANJA CAME TO THE TABLE WHERE MY COUSIN WAS SITTING...

AH. YOU WORK AT THE CARPENTRY SHOP. GO TO THE RIGHT.

SO WE GOT STAMPED OUR PASSPORTS AND CAME QUICK TO THE GOOD SIDE OF THE STADIUM. THOSE THEY SENT LEFT, THEY DIDN'T GET ANY STAMP.

"Torah Tales," from *Mendy and the Golem* (1987), scripted by Leibel Estrin, drawn by Dovid Sears. Reprinted by permission of the writer and artist.

WHEN THE DRIVER REACHED THE INN, THE BAAL SHEM TOV ASKED HIM WHAT HAD TAKEN PLACE...

"I TRIED TO BUY THE INNKEEPER'S WHISKEY," SAID THE DRIVER "BUT WE WOULD NOT AGREE ON A PRICE SO I LEFT..."

"WHEN I SAW THAT HE WOULDN'T BARGAIN, I TURNED AROUND AND PAID WHAT HE ASKED!"

THE BAAL SHEM TOV SMILED, "FROM HERE WE CAN LEARN ABOUT ONE OF THE MOST POWERFUL THINGS IN THE WORLD," HE SAID.

"YOU MEAN, THE POWER OF *WHISKEY?*" ASKED THE WAGON-DRIVER.

"SOMETHING EVEN *STRONGER!*" SAID THE BAAL SHEM TOV. " THE POWER OF TRUST IN *HASHEM!*"

THE END!

BOBBA SHIVA MACHLIA

"Family Tales" #1 by Marvin Friedman, from *Marvin Friedman* (New York: Jews, 2003). Reprinted by permission of the artist.

THEY HAD LITTLE REBA, THEN LITTLE SARAH, THEN LITTLE HARRY, THEN LITTLE TANIA, AND LITTLE SHPRINTZA, MY MOTHER FRANCES. THEY ALSO HAD A COUPLE OF BABIES THAT DIDN'T MAKE IT. A̶̶̶ AUNT SARAH TOLD ME THE FLOOR OF HER FATHER'S HOME WAS DIRT. DIRT! SORT OF HARD TO BELIEVE. BUT AUNT SARAH WAS THE LAST OF THE GREAT REMEMBERERS AND IT MUST BE SO. DIRT!

HONEST TO GOD, YOU NEVER BELIEVE YOU COULD
GO THROUGH THAT. WE ~~WAS~~ WAS ON THAT BOAT
FOR FOURTEEN DAYS. HERRING WAS HUNG
FROM A STRING. THAT WAS LUNCH AND DINNER.
A GYP. A REAL GYP. YOU COULD PAY ME A
MILLION DOLLARS, I WOULDN'T GO ON A BOAT
AGAIN.

I HAD LUNCH AT AUNT SARAH'S ~~AND~~ AND BETWEEN THE HERRING AND THE ENTENMANN'S ~~~~ COOKIES SHE TOLD ME, ~~~~ AWW, HONEY, YOUR DEAR FATHER, MAY HE REST IN PEACE, MET MY LITTLE SISTER, YOUR MOMMA, AND ONE, TWO, THREE, HE ~~~~ BROKE OFF HIS ENGAGEMENT TO ANNIE ~~~~ FEINSTEIN, TOOK BACK THE RING. IT WASN'T MUCH OF A RING, BUT IT WAS A RING. AND AWW, HONEY THAT ANNIE FEINSTEIN WAS HURT PRETTY BAD. BUT AZOY GAYT ISS, AND THAT WAS IT. HE DIDN'T HAVE A POT TO PEE IN, ~~~~ BUT YOUR MOMMA LOVED HIM AND THAT WAS IT. THEY WAS MARRIED BY RABBI LEVENTHOL IN HIS HOUSE IN PHILADELPHIA, AND, HONEY, THAT WAS IT. ~~~~ AWW, HONEY, YOU EAT LIKE A BIRD. ~~~~ I GOT A TASTYCAKE.

DON'T WORRY ABOUT ANNIE FEINSTEIN- SHE MARRIED SIDNEY MEESKEIT, A SHORT LITTLE MAN, BUT HE MADE A ~~~~ FORTUNE IN SHOWER CURTAINS. HE WAS NO SHEIK FROM ARABIA.

"The Mighty
Golem Swings" by
James Sturm, from
*America: God,
Gold and Golems*
(Montreal: Drawn
& Quarterly,
2007). Reprinted
by permission of
the artist.

①

Centerfielder stops the ball before it reaches the wall.

Mo scores on a high throw up the line. He pays a price — the catcher gives him a hard spike to his thigh.

If Mo's hurt he's not showing it. He's scored a run off Mickey McFadden.

McFadden is irate. He walks off the mound screaming into his glove.

Due to my knees I remain at first. Our clean-up hitter approaches the plate. The crowd becomes eerily quiet.

From *Berlin* #15 by Jason Lutes (Montreal: Drawn & Quarterly, 2008). Reprinted by permission of the artist.

"It's Only a Matter of Time" by Nicole Schulman, reprinted from *World War 3 Illustrated #37: Unnatural Disasters* (2006). Reprinted by permission of the artist.

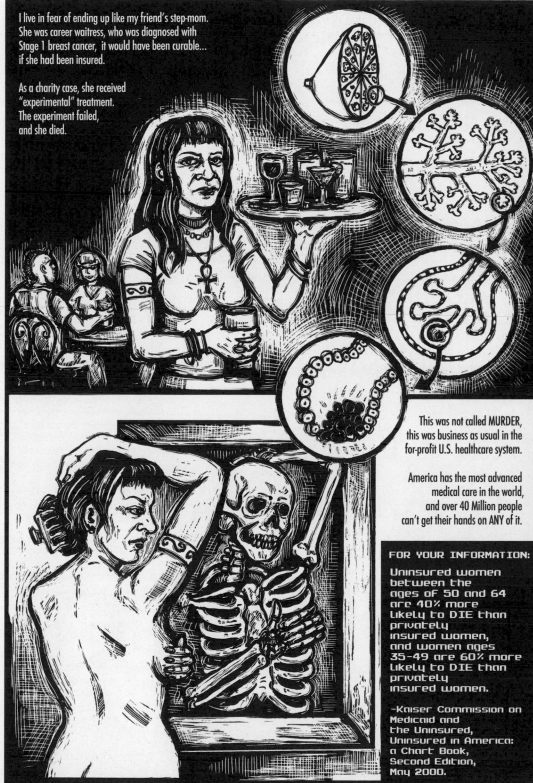

From *To the Heart of the Storm* (New York: Norton, 2000) by Will Eisner. Reprinted with the permission of the Eisner Estate.

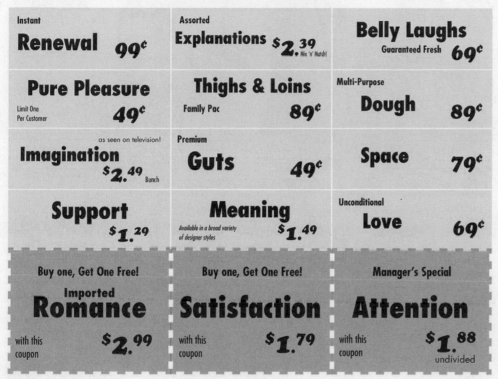

ON SALE TODAY!

Instant
Renewal 99¢

Assorted
Explanations $2.39 Mix 'n' Match!

Belly Laughs Guaranteed Fresh 69¢

Pure Pleasure
Limit One Per Customer 49¢

Thighs & Loins Family Pac 89¢

Multi-Purpose
Dough 89¢

as seen on television!
Imagination $2.49 Bunch

Premium
Guts 49¢

Space 79¢

Support $1.29

Meaning Available in a broad variety of designer styles $1.49

Unconditional
Love 69¢

Buy one, Get One Free!
Imported
Romance with this coupon $2.99

Buy one, Get One Free!
Satisfaction with this coupon $1.79

Manager's Special
Attention with this coupon $1.88 undivided

"Salvation for Sale" by Lawrence Bush. Reprinted from *America Torah Tunes* (Northvale, NJ: Jason Aronson, 2007) by permission of the artist.

"Leo Fuchs" written by Joel Schechter and drawn by Spain Rodriguez, from *Jewish Currents*, 2005. Reprinted with the artist's and writer's permission.

"Tzaruch Shemirah!" or Fish Story, written and drawn by Sara Rosenblum and David Lasky for the *Chicago Reader*. Reprinted by permission of the artists.

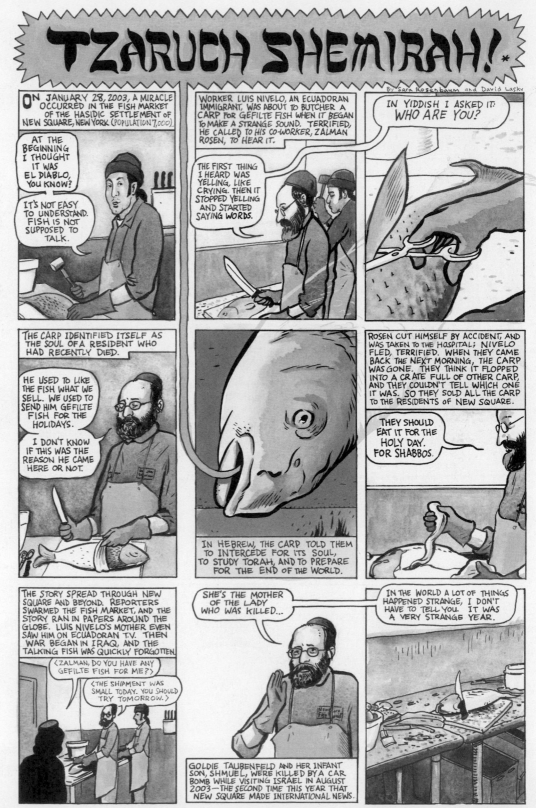

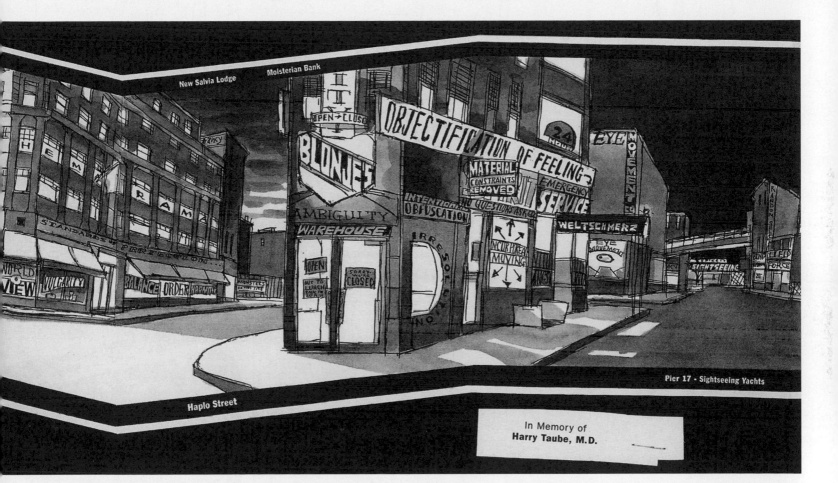

"Objectification of Feeling" by Ben Katchor, from *Julius Knipl, Real Estate Photographer* (New York: Pantheon Books, 2000). Used with permission of the artist.

"Free Associative House" by Ben Katchor, from *Julius Knipl, Real Estate Photographer*. Reprinted by permission of the artist.

168

169

From *We Are On Our Own* by Miriam Katin (Montreal:
Drawn & Quarterly, 2006). Copyright Miriam Katin;
used with permission of Drawn & Quarterly.

From "Jobnik, or Being a Woman in the Israeli Army" by Miriam Libicki, from *Jobnik #4* (self-published). Reprinted by permission of the artist.

"Ghost Stories" by Jeffrey Lewis, from *Fuff*, #4
(Spring 2006). Reprinted by permission of the artist.

From
"Lubavitch,
Ukraine,
1876" by
Sammy
Harkham
in *Kramer's
Ergot* 6 (Los
Angeles:
Buenaventura
Press and
Avodah
Books, 2006).
Reprinted by
permission of
the artist.

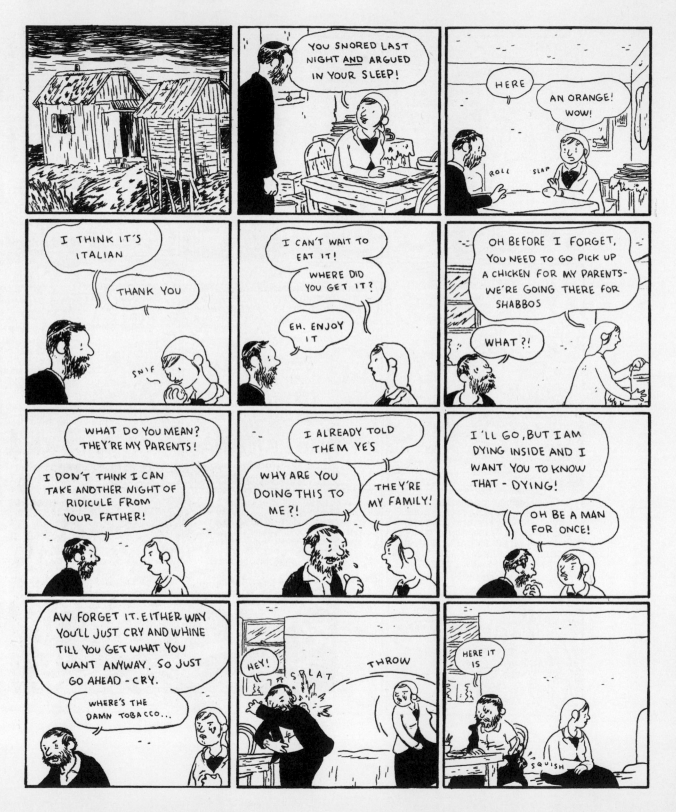

174

AND LITTLE DAVID WAS MADE KING

About the Contributors

LAWRENCE BUSH (1950–) edits *Jewish Currents* and was an editor of the arts journal *Jews*. He lives north of New York City.

MILTON CANIFF (1907–88) was one of the most celebrated of all daily comic strip artists and the creator of *Terry and the Pirates* and *Steve Canyon*. He was also one of the most commercially successful, ranking in his best years with Al Capp in million-fold readership.

AL CAPP (1909–79), arguably the most successful Jewish artist of the daily and Sunday press, was regarded as a "national treasure" of satire into the late 1950s.

ROBERT CRUMB (1943–), "King of the Undergrounds," according to his appellation in the 1970s, is a major figure in the modern history of comic and popular art. He lives in France and is at work on an adaptation of the biblical Book of Genesis.

JACK DAVIS (1924–) was born in Atlanta and was a GI Bill student at the University of Georgia; he took classes at the Art Students League and became one of the key artists of *Mad* comics, *Trump*, and *Humbug*. He is known for his advertising art, his drawings in *Time* and *TV Guide*, and especially his public-service drawings in later decades, including a 1989 U.S. postage stamp series honoring postal workers. He lives in New York.

KIM DEITCH (1944–), a pioneer of underground comix, edited *Gothic Blimp*, the comic tabloid of the *East Village Other*, in 1969; contributed to many comic anthologies; and in recent years has published several outstanding collections, including *The Boulevard of Broken Dreams* (2002) with his brother, Simon Deitch. He lives in New York.

ERIC DROOKER (1958–), a native New Yorker, was educated at Cooper Union, worked for two decades with the *World War 3 Illustrated* cooperative, and has published several books, including the memorable *Flood!* He now lives in Berkeley, California.

GARY DUMM (1947–), a Cleveland artist and frequent collaborator with Harvey Pekar, is the principal artist of *Students for a Democratic Society: A Graphic History*.

WILL EISNER (1907–2005), one of the giants of comic art, was among the first "packagers" of comic book contents for pulp publishers and was the inventor of *The Spirit*, a section of comic strips packaged with weekend editions of American newspapers. In his later years, he returned as a leading elder in the creation and the legitimation of art comics.

WILL ELDER (1921–), born Wolf Eisenberg in the Bronx, is arguably the greatest of all of *Mad*'s satirical artists. He drew much of the *Playboy* serial *Little Annie Fanny*, illustrated for many magazines, taught art, and painted. He lives in New Jersey.

LEIBEL ESTRIN (1949–) developed nineteen issues of *Mendy and the Golem*, several children's books, and dozens of articles around the themes that money, power, and worldly success deserve parody and ridicule and that ethical values are to health what air is to life. He collaborates with Dovid Sears and lives in Pittsburgh.

JULES FEIFFER (1929–), one of America's leading comic artists since the mid-1950s, has also been a playwright, screenwriter, and widely admired political commentator. He lives in New York.

BOB FINGERMAN (1964–) grew up in Queens, studied at the School of Visual Arts with Harvey Kurtzman, and collaborated with Kurtzman. He drew for the *Mad* knockoff *Cracked* for years and has created several books, including *Beg the Question*. He lives in New York.

MARVIN FRIEDMAN (1930–) grew up in Pennsylvania and lives in New York. His artwork has appeared frequently in the *New Yorker*, the *New York Times*, *Gourmet*, and *Good Housekeeping*, among other places. His book *Marvin Friedman* was published by the arts journal *Jews* in 2002. He lives in New Jersey.

RUBE GOLDBERG (1883–1970), the only comic artist whose name became an *Oxford English Dictionary* entry (a Rube Goldberg is a crazy, unnecessarily complicated invention), was in his later years a political cartoonist of note (and winner of a Pulitzer Prize on that account) and a leading figure in the professionalization of comics and cartooning.

LARRY GONICK (1946–), whose *Cartoon History of the Universe* is one of the enduring favorites of educational comic art, was educated in math at Harvard and has produced a series of outstanding popular explanations of science, along with his steady output of social satire.

JUSTIN GREEN (1945–), a major figure in underground comix, largely invented the autobiographical comic genre with the tortured saga of Binky Brown. His several books include *Musical Legends*, a compilation of pieces that originally appeared in *Pulse!* magazine. He and his wife, comic artist Carol Tyler, currently live in Ohio.

DAVID GREENBERGER (1954–) was born in Chicago and grew up in Erie, Pennsylvania. He later moved to Boston to attend the Massachusetts College of Art and began publishing *The Duplex Planet,* 1979. He's been living in upstate New York for the past couple of decades. The artist for "Heartburn and Heart Attack" is J.R. Williams (1957–). A painter, illustrator, sculptor, and animator, he is a native of Oregon living in the Portland area.

BILL GRIFFITH (1944–), named after his great-grandfather, nineteenth-century photographer William H. Griffith, is the famed artist of the daily *Zippy* strip, syndicated since 1986. He was an early underground comix artist and the co-editor, with Art Spiegelman, of *Arcade*, the most influential anthology of the genre. He grew up in Levittown and now lives, with his wife (and fellow artist), Diane Noomin, in Connecticut.

WILLIAM GROPPER (1897–1977), though not himself fluent in Yiddish, was among the favorite cartoonists of the left-wing Yiddish press. He became a prominent painter in the Works Progress Administration days of the New Deal, and despite suffering in the Red scare panic, he maintained a high reputation and loyal audience for his studio work.

MILT GROSS (1895–1953), creator of the first graphic novel in the United States, is better known as a comic novelist than a comic strip artist and is perhaps the best-remembered broken-English Jewish humorist in print.

SAMMY HARKHAM (1980–) was born in Los Angeles and later returned to that city from Australia. He has published several issues of *Kramer's Ergot*, one of the most highly regarded comic art anthologies, and several books of his own, including the prize-winning *Poor Sailor*.

HARRY HERSHFIELD (1885–1974), one of the giants of the comic strip in the first third of the twentieth century, was a newspaper celebrity columnist and a celebrity himself in radio and nightclubs.

LEON ISRAEL (1887–1955), the artist who dubbed himself "Lola," was the major original artistic contributor to the weekly *Groyser Kundes*, the supreme satirical magazine in the Yiddish language, published in New York, 1909–27, and a somewhat prominent painter.

BEN KATCHOR (1951–), son of a left-wing Yiddishist, is the recipient of Guggenheim and MacArthur fellowships and has drawn for the *Forward* newspaper, *Metropolis* magazine, and the *New Yorker*. In recent years, he has written several plays. He has nearly always lived in New York.

MIRIAM KATIN (1942–), a Holocaust survivor, left Hungary with her family for Israel in 1956. She has subsequently worked in Israeli animation and has drawn several children's books in New York, where she lives today.

MALCOLM KILDALE (d. 1971) was the creator and artist of numerous characters, the most prominent being Sgt. Spook and Speed Centaur. In 1941, he was hired by comics publisher Albert Lewis Kanter to adapt and illustrate *The Three Musketeers*, the first issue in the long-running *Classics Illustrated* series.

ALINE KOMINSKY (1948–), an escapee from Long Island and from art school, met Robert Crumb and became part of his artistic endeavors in 1970, later becoming his wife. She and Crumb lived for long stretches in Winters, California, and then the south of France, where the family remains. She has contributed to many comic publications, including *Dirty Laundry*, by herself and Crumb, and in recent years the *New Yorker*.

BERNARD KRIGSTEIN (1919–90), widely regarded as the most formally artistic of all comic book artists, drew for many companies until the mid-1950s, led a failed campaign to unionize comic book publishing, and later taught art and painted.

PETER KUPER (1958–) grew up in Cleveland, where he met Harvey Pekar and a visiting Robert Crumb; moved to New York in 1978; and worked on *Richie Rich* comics, co-founded *World War 3 Illustrated* with Seth Tobocman, and since 1997 has drawn the "Spy vs. Spy" feature for *Mad* magazine. He lives in New York when he is not in Mexico.

HARVEY KURTZMAN (1924–91) founder of *Mad* comics and a leading editor of war and action comic series at EC, founded several other satirical magazines (*Trump*, *Humbug*, and *Help!*) and scripted the *Playboy* feature *Little Annie Fanny*, which ran for two decades.

YOSEL KUTLER (1896–1935), one of the most talented of Yiddish comic artists, worked almost exclusively in left-wing publications and, with Zuni Maud, developed the Modikot puppet theater. His death in an automobile accident was seen as a terrible blow to the Yiddish theatrical (and left-wing) world.

DAVID LASKY (1967–) was raised in Virginia and moved to Seattle in 1992, where he joined a new wave of alternative cartoonists. He has since produced a number of experimental comic books and his art has appeared in a wide variety of anthologies. He collaborates with S.I. Rosenbaum.

JEFFREY LEWIS (1975–) grew up in New York's Lower East Side and his been a frequent contributor to *World War 3 Illustrated*. Besides writing and illustrating his own continuing comic series *Fuff*, he lives in New York and makes his living as a recording artist. You can learn more about his work at www.thejeffreylewissite.com.

MIRIAM LIBICKI (1981–) was born in Columbus, Ohio. After living in Jerusalem and Seattle, Washington, she is now based in Vancouver, Canada. She received a bachelor's degree in fine arts from the Emily Carr Institute in 2006 and is the creator of the comic series *Jobnik!* and the drawn essays *Towards a Hot Jew* and *Ceasefire*. Visit her artist Web site at www.realgonegirl.com.

JASON LUTES (1967–), born in New Jersey and raised mostly in Montana, graduated from the Rhode Island School of Design and worked at Fantagraphics in Seattle while beginning the series that became *Jar of Fools*. His series *Berlin* is regarded as crucial visual art about Weimar Germany shortly before Hitler's rise to power.

ZUNI MAUD (1881–1956), the only Yiddish comic artist to train formally (with the Art Students League in New York), reached the apex of his fame with the Modikot puppet troupe of the 1920s–30s. He drew extensively (cartoons, not comic strips) for the Yiddish newspaper *Morgn Frayhayt* in his later years.

SHELDON MAYER (1917–71), one of the forgotten giants of comic books' early years, "discovered" Superman for DC Comics, was a longtime editor at several firms and creator of two comic classics, the superhero satire *Scribbly* and the children's strip *Sugar and Spike*.

HARVEY PEKAR (1937–), scriptwriter for many comic art volumes, is the semi-fictive star of the much-lauded film *American Splendor* (2003). He lives in Cleveland.

SAUL RASKIN (1878–1966), who also worked under the name S. Raskin, was a versatile artist in the Yiddish newspapers best known for reworking existing comic images from a fresh angle.

TRINA ROBBINS (1937–) has been writing comics, books, and graphic novels for over thirty years. She lives in a dusty 105-year-old house in San Francisco with her books, shoes, and cats.

SPAIN RODRIGUEZ (1940–), best known for his creation Trashman and for his graphic biography of Che Guevara, was a founder of the underground comix movement and has remained prolific over the decades. He lives in San Francisco.

S.I. ROSENBAUM (1978–), a cartoonist and journalist from Boston, currently writes for the *St. Petersburg Times* in Florida and draws comics about Papua New Guinea. She collaborates with David Lasky.

SHARON RUDAHL (1947–), born in Virginia, was a civil rights activist and an artist for anti–Vietnam War underground newspapers and the feminist series *Wimmen's Comix*. She is known for her 2007 book *A Dangerous Woman: The Graphic Biography of Emma Goldman*. She lives in Los Angeles.

JOEL SCHECHTER (1947–), professor of theater arts at San Francisco State University, has written books about circus clowns and political satires. His most recent book, *Messiahs of 1933*, about American Yiddish theater, includes comic strips he wrote and Spain Rodriguez drew. He lives in San Francisco near the Doggie Diner.

NICOLE SCHULMAN (1975–) is an artist on the editorial board of *World War 3 Illustrated* magazine and co-editor of *Wobblies! A Graphic History*. Her work has been published and exhibited internationally, and is in the permanent collection of the Library of Congress. She was born, raised, and continues to live in New York City.

DOVID SEARS (1951–) attended the San Francisco Art Institute, worked as an abstract painter, and eventually turned to writing adult Judaica in the 1990s while practicing expressionist photography. He collaborates with Leibel Estrin and lives today in New York City.

ART SPIEGELMAN (1948–), raised in Queens, was an early underground cartoonist, a shaping editorial force as co-editor of *Arcade* and later *Raw*, won a special Pulitzer Prize in 1992 for *Maus*, and continues to produce astounding volumes. He lives in New York.

JAMES STURM (1965–), was a cartoonist for the *Daily Cardinal* at the University of Wisconsin, from which he graduated in 1986. He later received an MFA from the School of Visual Arts, co-founded the alternative tabloid *The Stranger*, worked on *Raw* magazine, and, in 2005, founded the Center for Cartoon Studies in White River Junction, Vermont.

SETH TOBOCMAN (1958–) grew up in Cleveland and published a comic fanzine with Peter Kuper, has lived in New York's Lower East Side since 1978, was active in anti-gentrification street agitation in various ways, has been a steady contributor to and editor of *World War 3 Illustrated*, and published several highly charged political art volumes.

ART YOUNG (1866–1943), a Gentile raised in nineteenth-century Wisconsin, was the leading American socialist cartoonist of the 1910s–30s, a victim of the wartime suppression of the radical magazine the *Masses*, and the supreme practitioner of the drawing method known as cross-hatching.

SAMUEL ZAGAT (1890–1964), the most successful Yiddish-language comic artist anywhere, became an illustrator for the *Jewish Daily Forward* and other publications after his comic strip days. He was also a distinguished photographer.

Superman was the creation of two Cleveland Jewish teenagers, artist JOE SHUSTER (1914–1992) and writer JERRY SIEGEL (1914–1996). They worked in comic books for decades afterward, and after protracted legal conflict, they failed to acquire rights to their iconic creation but they did receive substantial payments.

Batman was the creation of writer BOB KANE (born Robert Kahn, 1915–98) and artist BILL FINGER (1919–1979), two long-time professionals in the comics mainstream.

INTRODUCTION

1. Rube Goldberg had done remarkable comic strips in the past—as we shall see—but was mainly recognized as a cartoonist; he won a Pulitzer Prize in 1948, but for political cartooning.

2. David Zane Mairowitz and Robert Crumb, *Introducing Kafka* (Northampton, MA: Kitchen Sink, 1994). That such an extraordinary volume had a comics-specialist publisher (itself soon to leave the field, as Denis Kitchen reluctantly shifted to agenting and packaging) is yet more evidence of marginality. It has since been reprinted in the mainstream.

3. Detailed references appear throughout this book to volumes bearing on Jewish comics and other useful works. Paul Buhle's "The New Scholarship of Comics" (*Chronicle of Higher Education*, May 16, 2003) was a shot across the bow: the notion of scholarship, if not much scholarship itself, had finally surfaced within the wider academic community after decades of essays and reviews in the *Comics Journal*, among other places. Several of the excellent fan-based scholarly volumes referenced here had already appeared, and in the years since, the pace of scholarly investigation and publication has been accelerating greatly.

4. See Anne Elizabeth Moore and Chris Ware, eds., *The Best American Comics 2007* (Boston: Houghton Mifflin, 2007), xiii–xxiv.

5. Ibid., xxi.

6. David Roskies, *A Bridge of Longing: The Lost Art of Yiddish Storytelling* (Cambridge, MA: Harvard University Press, 1995). Roskies clearly mistrusts the popular culture aura of Sholem Aleichem and other Yiddish greats as being both suspiciously left-wing and indifferent to the visionary project of a Jewish state. Dovid Katz has provided a different and more sympathetic account of the founding Yiddishists as literary masters bringing together different strains of Jewish culture; see Katz, *Words on Fire: The Unfinished Story of Yiddish* (New York: Perseus/Basic, 2004), 238–46, 257–71.

7. Sander Gilman, *The Jew's Body* (New York: Routledge, 1991), 134–36.

8. Ibid., 152, 192, 235–36.

9. Comic strips in the *Times* proper actually have made an intermittent appearance since the mid-1990s. The artists have been Jewish (Peter Kuper was the most frequently featured) or the artistic collaborators of Harvey Pekar. The Entertainment section and the Op-Ed pages have provided the space; a comics *page* remains unthinkable. The appearance of comics in the magazine section in 2006 was nevertheless a major marker. None of the newest comic artists so far in the *Times Magazine* pages, however, include Jewish content, although Daniel Clowes was among the earliest artists serialized.

10. Paul Buhle, ed., *Jews and American Popular Culture* (Westport, CT: Praeger/ Greenwood, 2007), three volumes, is the first systematic effort at tackling this broad subject.

11. But had it ever been as solid as it seemed? Paul Kriwaczek, in *Yiddish Civilization: The Rise and Fall of a Forgotten Nation* (New York: Vintage, 2005), argues that the currents creating Jewishness, ancient to modern, flowed from so many directions that genetic claims are inherently dubious, and the reality of Jewish culture lies within the flow itself.

12. *Squa Tront*, an EC fanzine, has been on the job for thirty years, intermittently. But with Gary Groth and Greg Sadowski, eds., *Will Elder: The Mad Playboy of Art* (Seattle: Fantagraphic Books, 2003); Bhob Stewart, ed., *Against the Grain: Mad Artist Wallace Wood* (Raleigh, NC: Twomorrows Publishing, 2003); and most of all Greg Sadowski, *B. Krigstein* (Seattle: Fantagraphic Books, 2002), the field of scholarship has gained real maturity.

13. See the highly useful overview by Paul von Blum, "Justice, Justice You Shall Pursue: Jewish Political Artists," in Buhle, *Jews and American Popular Culture*, vol. II, 151–82.

14. John Berger, *About Looking* (New York: Pantheon, 1980), 158.

15. Most fully expressed in Franklin Rosemont, ed., *Surrealism and Its Popular Accomplices* (San Francisco: City Lights, 1982), which originally appeared as an issue of the journal published by myself, *Cultural Correspondence*.

16. A fall 2007 exhibit opening in Paris was called "De Superman au Chat du Rabbin" (From Superman to the Rabbi's Cat); it was moved to the Joods Historisch Museum in Amsterdam in 2008, retitled "Superheros and Schlemiels: Jewish Memory in Comic Strip Art." The catalog/booklet is entitled *Du Superman au Chat du rabbin: Les juifs et la bandedessinée, Musée d'art et d'histoire du Judaïsme* (Paris, 2007). The last exhibit with such aims was held at the Cartoon Research Library, Ohio State University, June 28–Sept. 3, 1999; called "Jewish Cartoonists and the American Experience," it addressed itself very largely to cartoons and not strips, but made an interesting beginning with a short catalog essay by Helen Schlam. The artists represented were: Al Capp, Will Eisner, Jules Feiffer, Rube Goldberg, Harry Hershfield, Al Hirschfeld, Ben Katchor, Mell Lazarus, David Levine, Paul Palnik, Art Spiegelman, Hilda Terry, Jerry Siegel, Stan Mack, and Saul Steinberg. Of these, the only identifiably Jewish subjects were in pieces by Harry Hershfield, Ben Katchor, Art Spiegelman, Stan Mack, and the little-known Ohio artist Paul Palnik. An exhibit based upon work in the current volume opens at the John Nicholas Brown Gallery at Brown University in November 2008.

CHAPTER 1: YELLOW PRESS HEADLINERS: JEWISH COMICS IN THE DAILIES

1. Scholarship of the Yiddish comics is practically nonexistent. But see Eddy Portnoy and Paul Buhle, "Comic Strips/Comic Books," in *Jews and American Popular Culture*, vol. 2 (Westport, CT: Praeger/Greenwood, 2007), ed. Paul Buhle, 314–17.

2. Occasionally there was a momentary comeback, as in the antireligious one-shot satirical publication of *Boydek Khomets* by Yiddishists in 1934; it is reprinted here with a notable strip by Maud's frequent collaborator Yosel Kutler. The title literally means "Search for Leaven," referring to the cleaning out of the dwelling before Passover, and refers here to workers cleaning the global household of Nazism, but also of religious obscurantism.

3. John J. Appel, "Abie the Agent, Gimpl the Matchmaker, Berl Schlemazel, et al.," *Midstream* 28 (January 1988), especially 13–14.

4. See Maynard Frank Wolfe, *Rube Goldberg: Inventions* (New York: Simon & Schuster, 2000).

5. Joe Palooka was taken up for B films as early as 1934, with Jimmy Durante cast as Joe's manager, then shifted into a left-wing-staffed series of bottom-dollar films exhibiting the foibles of capitalist society. See Paul Buhle and Dave Wagner, *Radical Hollywood* (New York: The New Press, 2002), 149, n. 35.

6. See the keen remarks by Pete Hamill in "Milton Caniff," in John Carlin, ed., *Masters of American Comics* (Los Angeles: Hammer Museum, and New Haven: Yale University Press, 2005), 229–36.

7. See the informative volume edited by leading Caniff scholar Robert C. Harvey, *Milton Caniff: Conversations* (Jackson, MS: University Press of Mississippi, 2002).

8. M. Thomas Inge, *Comics as Culture* (Jackson: University Press of Missouri, 1990), 66.

9. Special thanks to Denis Kitchen for these insights into Al Capp.

10. Thanks for this observation go to Danny Fingeroth, director of *Spider-Man* at Marvel Comics for a decade, who pointed this out in a note to the author, May 18, 2007.

CHAPTER 2: COMIC BOOK HEROES

1. Gerard Jones, *Men of Tomorrow: Geeks, Gangsters, and the Birth of the Comic Book* (New York: Basic Books, 2004), 1–40.

2. Gershon Legman would later insist that the key influence upon the two Cleveland Jews was fascistic, even Nazi-like. A better argument could be made (and has often been made) for a Nietzschean factor, but blue-joke specialist Legman was writing a polemic. See the excerpt from his screed in Jeet Heer and Kent Worcester, eds., *Arguing Comics: Literary Masters on a Popular Medium* (Jackson, MS: University of Mississippi Press, 2005), 112–21.

3. Mayer created the funniest of the 1930s superhero satires, with a genuinely heroic housewife in long underwear halting crime, and went on, after his editing years, to create an endearing kids' strip, *Sugar and Spike*. See "Sheldon Mayer, Memories of a Comics Legend," *Comics Journal* 148 (February 1992), 91–96.

4. Among the various fan-oriented studies, *The Steranko History of Comics*, vol. 2 (Reading, PA: Supergraphics, 1972) has a fine description of comic book characters during the 1930s–40s, with details on the work of some outstanding, now

largely forgotten, artists such as Lou Fine. Author James Steranko is himself a central figure in superhero comics.

5. Interview with Harvey Kurtzman, Columbia University Oral History Program, 1991. See also Denis Kitchen and Paul Buhle, *The Art of Harvey Kurtzman* (New York: Abrams, 2009), for many details of Kurtzman's life and work.

6. Gerard Jones, *Men of Tomorrow*, 197–98, 202–03.

7. Danny Fingeroth, *Disguised as Clark Kent: Jews, Comics, and the Creation of the Superhero* (New York: Continuum, 2007), 58–60. Many comic superheroes actually had dark hair, if no notable Semitic visual hints, and Captain America darkened his locks in a 1970s reinvention.

8. Of a number of sources, one of the best is the Web site Dan Markstein's Toonopedia, www.toonopedia.com/crimepay.htm. See also Ron Goulart, *The Comic Book Reader's Companion* (New York: Harper's, 1993), 39–41; Alex C. Malloy, ed., *Comic Book Artists* (Radnor, PA: Wallace-Homestead Book Company, 1993), 62–63; and Hubert H. Crawford, *Crawford's Encyclopedia of Comic Books* (Middle Village, NY: Jonathan David Publishers, Inc), 231–62, including a poor-quality reprint of several strips from various Lev Gleason books. Gleason actually published a leftish knockoff of *Reader's Digest* called *Reader's Scope* from 1943 to 1946, with Truman Capote among the regular contributors. It was the demise of this magazine, as the Cold War closed doors, that apparently prompted Gleason to turn his full attention to comics.

9. Will Eisner later insisted that he had originated the idea of Classics: based upon the success of literary adaptations in contemporary Europe, he created *Education Comics*, couldn't sell copies, then sold the idea of Classics to Kantor. See Diana Schutz and Denis Kitchen, eds., *Will Eisner's Shop Talk* (Milwaukie, OR: Dark Horse, 2001), 324. See also William B. Jones Jr., *Classics Illustrated: A Cultural History, with Illustrations* (Jefferson, NC: McFarland & Company, 2002).

10. My account of the Red scare in Hollywood and its full implications in the popular culture of the 1940s–70s is given in two volumes, both written with Dave Wagner: *Radical Hollywood* and *Hide in Plain Sight* (New York: Palgrave, 2003).

11. This story is told somewhat differently, but thoroughly, in David Hajdu, *The Ten-Cent Plague* (New York: Farrar, Strauss and Giroux, 2008), 245–318.

12. Jones, *Men of Tomorrow*, 263–64.

13. The tale of those liberal filmmakers, nearly all Jewish, and their monster/sci-fi films is also related in Paul Buhle and Dave Wagner, *Hide in Plain Sight*, 69–84.

14. See Denis Kitchen and Paul Buhle, *The Art of Harvey Kurtzman*, for the best account.

15. Among the finest of the volumes on all individual comic artists thus far is Greg Sadowski, *B. Krigstein*, from which the following details are derived.

16. Gaines's testimony is reprinted in "The Senate Subcommittee Testimony," in *Tales of Terror!* (Seattle: Fantagraphics, 2000 edition), 21–27.

17. Ironically, some of best of those Southern-novel adaptations for film were directed by Martin Ritt, who shared much of Kurtzman's background and world-view but had gone to college in the South en route to a distinguished career in television and films. See Buhle and Wagner, *Hide in Plain Sight*, 186–88.

18. Rubinstein also did the adaptation of a rare revised edition of a Classic, the 1956 version of *A Tale of Two Cities*, likewise drawn by Orlando. Out of work but on the road lecturing, Rubinstein did more adaptations, under various names, but when interviewed by myself on details decades later, she was unsure about which were further adapted by other hands and published.

19. See Julia Mickenberg, *Learning from the Left: Children's Literature, the Cold War, and Radical Politics in the United States* (New York: Oxford University Press, 2006).

20. William B. Jones Jr., *Classics Illustrated*, 187–89. Graphic Classics is an anthology series published in Mt. Horeb, Wisconsin, based upon authors whose works are in the public domain and, like Poe or H.G. Wells, have been of wide interest to a popular audience. Graphic Classics' circulation is, of course, small by contrast to the huge readership of the original but they may be considered the proper successor nevertheless.

21. See Gary Groth, "The Jules Feiffer Interview," in *Comics Journal* 124 (August 1988), especially 38–45. Feiffer trained with Will Eisner, among others, and remained grateful for the apprenticeship. An extended interview about his early days with Eisner was published in an obscure fanzine: see "Jules Feiffer Talks About the Spirit," *Panels* 1 (1979), 22–23 (the interview was presumably conducted by the fanzine's editor/publisher, John Benson). Feiffer's recounting of his own youthful attachment to comics has been reprinted as Feiffer, *The Great Comic Book Heroes* (Seattle: Fantagraphics, 2003).

22. See Mike Benton, *The Comic Book in America: An Illustrated History*, 2nd ed. (Dallas: Taylor Publishing Company, 1993), especially 53–70. See also Glen David Gold, "Lo, from the Demon Shall Come—the Public Dreamer!!!" in *Masters of American Comics*, 258–67.

CHAPTER 3: THE UNDERGROUND ERA

1. According to a widely held view of underground comix history, the very first after Jack Jackson's 1964 theologically inspired satire, *God Nose*, was a pamphlet-format satire on Lenny Bruce, *Lenny of Laredo* (1965), self-published by Berkeley artist Joel Beck and distributed in a later edition by the Print Mint, the first comic printed by that Berkeley poster business.

2. A small variety of local counterculture magazines featured the work of nascent underground cartoonists. Among these, the *Chicago Mirror*, which published its premiere issue in Autumn 1967, is representative, and with its center-spread LSD strip by Art Spiegelman (unsigned), its nudie photo, and its mixture of poetry and antiestablishment articles, it marked a transition from college humor magazines toward the underground press. Some of its contributors would continue on to the *Chicago Seed*, a major avenue for comics and hippie perspectives.

3. Jack Jackson (aka Jaxon) was the main artist here, and none of the collaborators happened to be Jewish.

4. Some of this story is told in Paul Buhle, *From the Lower East Side to Hollywood: Jews in American Popular Culture* (New York: Verso, 2004), 173–76.

5. Dez Skinn, *Comix: The Underground Revolution* (New York: Thunder's Mouth Press, 2004), 20–22, makes the somewhat different argument that the underground press illustrations pointed the way. The views are not mutually exclusive.

6. R. Crumb interview by Paul Buhle, from *Cultural Correspondence* 5 (Summer/Fall 1977), 10–12, reprinted in Buhle, ed., *Popular Culture in America* (Minneapolis: University of Minnesota Press, 1990), 172.

7. One of the best but least-appreciated volumes on the history of the undergrounds is Bob Levin, *The Pirates and the Mouse: Disney's War Against the Counterculture* (Seattle: Fantagraphics, 2003).

8. Trina Robbins offered her sharpest comments, ironically enough, in Monte Beauchamp, ed., *The Life and Times of R. Crumb* (New York: St. Martins/Griffin, 1998), 41–42.

9. "Kim Deitch Interviewed by Monte Beauchamp," *Comics Journal* 123 (July 1988), 56–62.

10. Ibid., 64–69.

11. Sharon Rudahl, *A Dangerous Woman: The Graphic Biography of Emma Goldman* (New York: The New Press, 2007). I am the editor of this volume.

12. Stanley Wiater and Stephen R. Bissette, "Harvey Pekar and Joyce Brabner: By the People, for the People," in Wiater and Bissette, eds., *Comic Book Rebels: Conversations with the Creators of the New Comics* (New York: Donald J. Fine, 1993), 131.

13. It is notable that early scholarship on Pekar and his comics was inclined to overlook his Jewishness entirely. See Joseph Witek, *Comic Books as History: The Narrative Art of Jack Jackson, Art Spiegelman, and Harvey Pekar* (Jackson, MS: University Press of Mississippi, 1989).

14. An apparent commercial breakthrough, which promptly fell through. *Comix Book* (1974), edited by Denis Kitchen, published by Stan Lee, and featuring the work of leading underground artists— including one of Art Spiegelman's first postmodern strips, "Ace Hole, Midget Detective"—only lasted two issues. Thus did *Arcade* become the last anthological resort of the undergrounders.

15. Green's collection of comics, *Musical Legends* (San Francisco: Last Gasp, 2004), taken from his drawings in *Pulse!* magazine, contains a healthy dose of the Jewish idols, mostly fallen idols, of the music world. His tracing of Mike Bloomfield shows a close affiliation with the subject.

16. *Comics Journal* 180 and 181, September and October, 1995; reprinted in *The New Comics*, edited by Gary Groth and Robert Fiore (New York: Berkeley Books, 1988).

17. The first major undergound comix historical exhibit (after a half-dozen smaller versions) is scheduled for the Chazen Museum of Madison, Wisconsin, in April 2009, with an exhibit volume, to be published by Abrams, edited by Denis Kitchen and James Danky.

18. Thierry Smolderen, "Of Labels, Loops and Bubbles," *Comic Art* 12 (Summer 2006), 112.

CHAPTER 4: RECOVERING JEWISHNESS

1. Of all the related effects, *Considering Maus: Approaches to Art Spieglman's "Survivor's Tale" of the Holocaust* (Tuscaloosa: University of Alabama Press, 2003), edited by Deborah R. Geis, is arguably the most old-fashioned, i.e., a strictly academic volume. And yet it also marks the "Jewish touch," the ascent into scholarship with mostly, not entirely, Jewish scholars. A CD-ROM entitled *The Compleat Maus* had already been released in 1994, the year of the MoMA exhibit. See also the page-one commentary in the *New York Times Book Review*

by David Hajdu entitled "Homeland Insecurity," a review of *In the Shadow of No Towers*. I wish to acknowledge being a panelist for the *Maus* exhibit at the Jewish Museum in Philadelphia: the enlarged panels had an emotional impact upon me as well.

2. R.C. Harvey, "Masters of American Comics: Put This in Your Canon and Shoot It Off," *Comics Journal* 282 (April 2007), 178, 184–85.

3. Harvey, "Masters," 178.

4. Kent Worcester, "NYC Feiffer Exhibit Draws Participation of Chast, Kuper, Modell, Sorel, Spiegelman, Trudeau," *Comics Journal* 253 (June 2003), 35–36.

5. Thierry Smolderen, "Of Labels, Loops and Bubbles," 90–113.

6. Pekar, at a forum called "Comics and Culture" at Brown University, April 14, 2007.

7. See Avram Kampf, *Jewish Experience in the Art of the Twentieth Century* (South Hadley, MA: Bergin and Harvey, 1984), 63–64.

8. Among other developments among the Fantastic Four, the Thing, aka Benjamin Jacob Grimm, identified himself as Jewish in 2002, as noted by Simcha Weinstein in *Up, Up and Oy Vey!* (Baltimore: Leviathan Books, 2006), 75.

9. Danny Fingeroth, *Disguised as Clark Kent: Jews, Comics, and the Creation of the Superhero*, 97–104.

10. Will Eisner, "Joe Simon," in *Will Eisner's Shop Talk*, 335.

11. See his interview, "Men in Tights," in *The New Comics*, edited by Gary Groth and Robert Fiore, 81–93. Another interesting artist in this regard is Greg Rucka, who came from a left-liberal family in Salinas, California. See Andrew Farago, "The Greg Rucka Interview," in *Comics Journal* 287 (January 2008), 67–88.

12. Danny Fingeroth, *Disguised as Clark Kent*, 108.

13. Thanks to a note from Danny Fingeroth, May 28, 2007, for this observation. His book details the assorted Jewish comic artists in the mainstream, with trenchant notes on their work. See also Dana Jennings, "At House of Comics, a Writer's Champion," *New York Times*, September 15, 2003, a characteristic evocation of the new direction of graphic novel sales and the editor at Vertigo (DC's imprint) who makes it happen: Karen Berger. Harvey Pekar is prominent in this well-paying line.

14. Notable print trade exception: Bobby London, from the Air Pirates crowd of the 1970s, took his strip featuring a Groucho Marx–like character named Dirty Duck first to the *National Lampoon* but later to *Playboy*, where it has appeared for a quarter century. That said, he also worked on *The SpongeBob SquarePants*

Movie, and his major comics entry of recent years was tucked into a Ramones record as an extra.

15. See Gary Groth, "Bill Griffith Interview," *Comics Journal* 157 (March 1993), 52–98.

16. The breakthrough essay for Katchor's public reputation was Lawrence Wechsler, "Profile: A Wanderer in the Perfect City," *New Yorker*, August 9, 1993, 58–66.

17. Geis, *Considering Maus*, 3.

18. Spiegelman was to say later, about *No Towers*, that it "expresses my secular diasporist, Jewish nature"; see Michael Dooley and Steven Heller, eds., *The Education of a Comics Artist* (New York: Allworth Press, 2005), 112. Among his later works is a children's story, "Prince Rooster," based on a Hasidic folk tale, in *Big Fat Little Lit* (New York: Puffin Books, 2003), edited by Spiegelman and Françoise Mouly, 27–32. A wise old man with a beard looks suspiciously like Crumb's Mr. Natural.

19. Zwigoff's next film was *Ghost World* (2001), a rendition of a comic strip narrative by Dan Clowes about a Jewish teenager's alienation as she graduates from high school with one main interest (apart from not being bored): cartooning. It was, in parts, very touching.

20. See especially *The Cartoon History of the Universe* (San Francisco: RipOff Press, 1978). Thanks to Larry Gonick for an e-mail message. Since his underground days, Gonick has published two-score volumes of popularizations, largely of history and science.

21. Peter Kuper, *The Metamorphosis* (New York: Crown, 2003).

22. Seth Tobocman, *Disaster and Resistance: Political Comics* (Oakland: AK Press, 2008).

23. See Kent Worcester, "Waxing Politics with Seth Tobocman," *Comics Journal* 233 (May 2001), 78–102. *War in the Neighborhood: A Graphic Novel* (New York: Autonomedia, 1999) is really a record of what he saw and did, somewhat fictionalized but captured in all its dynamic energies and many of its internal contradictions (such as the inability of substance abusers to become communitarians in the squat community).

24. Eric Drooker, *Street Posters* (New York: Seven Stories Press, 1998).

25. See Tom Spurgeon, "The James Sturm Interview," *Comics Journal* 251 (1999), 77–115. Sturm noticeably avoided "Jewish" comments even about "The Golem's Mighty Swing."

26. Thanks to Jason Lutes for helpful observations about himself in e-mail communications.

27. Jason Lutes and Nick Bertozzi, *Houdini: The Handcuff King* (New York: Hyperion, 2007), another in the Center for Cartoon Studies volumes.

28. "Lubavitch, Ukraine, 1876," first published in *Kramer's Ergot* 6 (2006), edited by Sammy Harkham, then reprinted for a wider audience in *The Best American Comics 2007* (Boston: Houghton Mifflin, 2007), edited by Chris Ware, 121–31. *Mendy and the Golem*, written by Leibel Estrin and drawn by Dovid Sears, self-proclaimed the "world's only kosher comic," began as a strip serialized in some Jewish newspapers in the late 1970s but had nineteen issues published in two one-year series, in 1981 and 2003. The stories were largely taken from Hasidic lore and featured the Wonder Rabbis of the Pale in old times. The second series tended more toward freewheeling satire, without losing its *frumeh*, or pious quality. Meanwhile, a small stream of graphic-novel-like Torah books are largely aimed at Jewish children. The most distinguished artist's work is in Joe Kubert, *The Adventures of Yaacov and Isaac* (Tampa: Mahrwood Press, 2004).

29. See Ariel Schrag, ed., *Stuck in the Middle: Seventeen Comics from an Unpleasant Age* (New York: Viking, 2007); Vanessa Davis and Lauren Weinstein are also published together with other artists in *Best American Comics 2007*.

30. See Albert Fried, "The Story of America's Jewish Gangsters," a fresh look at the topic by the author of a foundational work on the subject of decades earlier, in Paul Buhle, ed., *Jews in American Popular Culture*, vol. 3 (Westport: Praeger/Greenwood, 2007), 181–200; Joe Kubert, *Jew Gangster* (New York: iBooks, 2006); Neil Kleid and Jake Allen, *Brownsville: A Graphic Novel* (New York: NMB, 2006); and Miriam Katin, *We Are on Our Own* (Montreal: Drawn & Quarterly, 2006).

31. Holocaust graphic novels by younger generations seem certain to increase, along with graphic novels about specifically Jewish characters' illnesses and disabilities, as well as the more expected Torah lessons and characterizations of anti-Semitism.

32. *From Aargh! to Zap! Harvey Kurtzman's Visual History of the Comics* (New York: Byron Preiss, 1991), 92. The ailing Kurtzman's assisting author was Michael Barrier.

Contributor and Art List

AUTHOR	TITLE	PUBLICATION	YEAR	PAGE
Lawrence Bush	"Salvation for Sale"	*Torah Tunes*	2007	163
Milton Caniff	"Terry and the Pirates"	syndicated strip	1946	47
Al Capp	"Li'l Abner"	syndicated strip	1946	48
R. Crumb	"Pa-Ayper-Reggs!!"	*The New American Splendor Anthology*	1993	14–15
	"What Superman Means to Me"	*Snarf*	1989	70–72
	"Dale Steinberger, The Jewish Cowgirl"	*Big Ass Comix*	1969	99
	"Lenore Goldberg and Her Girl Commandos"	*City Comix*	1969	101–03
	"Let's Have a Little Talk"	*Dirty Laundry*	1979	108
Jack Davis	"What's My Shine?"	*Mad Comics*	1954	78
Kim Deitch	"Little Kimbo in Pinkoland"	*Raw Magazine*	1991	86
Eric Drooker	"David and Goliath"	*World War 3 Illustrated*	1988	140–41
	"JEWBLACK"	*World War 3 Illustrated*	1992	144
Gary Dumm	"What Superman Means to Me"	*Snarf*	1989	70–72
	"My Struggle with Corporate Corruption and Network Philistinism"	*The New American Splendor Anthology*	1993	110–112
Will Eisner	"To the Heart of the Storm"	excerpt	2000	162
Will Elder	"Special Art Issue"	*Mad Comics*	1955	79
	"Twenty-Win"	*Humbug*	1958	82–84